HOW TO GET BETTER REVIEWS FOR YOUR FIRST NOVEL

HOW TO GET BETTER REVIEWS FOR YOUR FIRST NOVEL

11 Convos on the Basics of Fiction Writing for New Self-publishing Authors

By

Harold A. Bascom

NOVELIST & REVIEWER OF SELF-PUBLISHED FICTION

Copyright © 2018 Harold A. Bascom. All rights reserved.

No part of this publication may be reproduced, distributed, or transmitted in any form or by any means, including photocopying, recording, or other electronic or mechanical methods, without the prior written permission of the publisher, except in the case of brief quotations embodied in reviews and certain other noncommercial uses permitted by copyright law. The information provided within this book is for general information purposes only. While the author tries to keep the information up-to-date and correct, there are no representations or warranties, express or implied, about the completeness, accuracy, reliability, suitability or availability with respect to the information contained in this book for any purpose. Any use of this information is at your own risk. Any advice that is provided in this book is based on the experience of the author and does not reflect the opinion of Amazon. All opinions expressed in this book, are solely the opinions of the author.

DISCLAIMER:

The author/publisher of this book is not an accredited instructor in the field of fiction writing. The contents of this compilation of articles are drawn from the author/publisher's 30-plus years of experience in the field of fiction writing. The methods described in this book are the author/publisher's personal thoughts. They are not intended to be a definitive set of instructions for new creative writers. You may discover there are other methods and approaches to accomplish the same result. As such, the author/publisher is providing this book and its contents on an "as is" basis and makes no guarantees of any kind with respect to this book or its contents. Your purchase and use of this book imply your acceptance of this disclaimer.

COVER DESIGN & GRAPHICS BY HAROLD A. BASCOM

For new crafters of fiction everywhere

"Start writing, no matter what.
The water does not flow until
the faucet is turned on."

— Louis L'Amour

TABLE OF CONTENTS

- **Preface** — Page **1.**
- CONVO #1: How to protect that novel you're writing from crappy reviews — Page **3.**
- CONVO #2: 5 things you need to take into consideration before sending your manuscript to a developmental editor — Page **15.**
- CONVO #3: How to prevent your novel from possibly being tossed because of one inappropriate word in it — Page **29.**
- CONVO #4: An introduction to choosing points of view and how tenses affect them — Page **37.**
- CONVO #5: Fiction writing is a craft. There's no doubt about it — Page **47.**
- CONVO #6: How an acting lesson can help your dialogue in fiction — Page **61.**
- CONVO #7: How to write great descriptive scenes by employing the 5 human senses — Page **67.**
- CONVO #8: Would the story of your life make a bestselling book? — Page **71.**
- CONVO #9: How to find the art in rewriting — Page **81.**
- CONVO #10: Cliché hunting: How to identify them in your writing and fix them with extreme prejudice — Page **91.**
- CONVO #11: Where do ideas for plots of short stories and novels come from? — Page **99.**
- SUPPLEMENT: About my graphic illustrations — Page **123.**
- ABOUT THE AUTHOR — Page **131.**

PREFACE

I am just a regular guy who became a published novelist. It happened because there was a burning need in me to tell stories. But I had to know how one became a writer and began reading about the process. I learned that to write well one needed to read a lot—especially the kind of books one intended to write. I began reading voraciously, and in the year 1980, I started writing a novel based on a manhunt in Guyana, South America.

The first pages were pathetic; the grammar and composition were bad, and I knew I had to fix my shortcomings—all of which sprang from me not understanding the basics of fiction writing. I hit the libraries and delved into quite a few titles on the writers' craft. A key reference amongst them was *The Elements of Style* by William Strunk, Jr., and E. B. White. Soon, my writing began to improve. In 1983 I submitted my first manuscript to Heinemann Educational Books of London, and three years later my first novel, *APATA: The Story of a Reluctant Criminal* was published. I have not ceased writing since. As such, I have been a writer for thirty-plus years. Between that time and now I continue to improve on my literary crafting.

Currently, I review novels and short-story-collections put out by independent presses and self-published authors. In this role, I continue to come across ineptly crafted stories that I continue to give low review-ratings. Most of the latter, I suspect, were written by individuals led to believe writing was easy—a quick hustle to make some passive income. But writing is not easy as skating on ice is not easy. One who has never skated before does not strap on ice skates for the first time and do pirouettes on a rink. It is the same with writing fiction: one who has never written a scene with tight, compelling dialogue or an engaging descriptive paragraph does not open a blank document and start writing a best-selling novel. There are basics in learning to skate as there are basics in learning to write.

This book presents eleven articles (hopefully unpretentious on my part and often informal in tone) that I call 'convos' (conversations) that introduce and reinforce some of the fundamentals that need to be understood and applied in fiction writing. In short, this title is calculated to help you, a beginning writer planning to self-publish, put out a much better manuscript. I hope it turns out valuable for you.

CONVO #1:

How to Protect That Novel You're Writing from Crappy Reviews

A key reason one novel receives a one-star review while another gets top stars always boils down to the story-crafting of each. A novel written by an author who does not fully grasp the technical basics of writing fiction is the one likely to get that one-star review.

(But before I speak in depth about strategies you can employ to protect your story from bad reviews, let me list the three kinds of editors that are employed by any given traditional publishing company. First, there is the **DEVELOPMENTAL EDITOR**; this individual is also called a 'story editor.' After the developmental editor is finished working with the author, there is the **COPY EDITOR** whose job is to work with the writer to fix anything that is off grammatically; they also look at punctuation and spelling. And then there is the **PROOFREADER**; this is a kind of editor who catches and does a markup through the manuscript of any typos and errors in grammar or punctuation the copy editor might have missed. The latter is the final step before the manuscript is sent off to be printed as a novel.)

So, how do you protect that manuscript you're working on from becoming one of those painful-to-read, self-published titles out there? The answer is simple: Work with a developmental editor. (From here on, **D.E.** stands for Developmental Editor.) You may have to pay for developmental editing, and it would be worth every penny. If, however, your budget puts you beyond the reach of hiring one, the good news is, I'm going to show you, in this convo, how you may be able to find developmental editing for free. I'll be starting, however, from detailing what a D.E. is *and what they do. I'll speak on the key differences between a beta reader and a developmental editor. I will touch on the importance of inculcating the mindset of a D.E., how to have a good relationship with one—and more. I promise you; this will be a very comprehensive conversation.*

HOW TO PROTECT THAT NOVEL YOU'RE WRITING FROM CRAPPY REVIEWS

SO, WHO EXACTLY ARE DEVELOPMENTAL EDITORS, AND WHAT DO THEY DO?

A developmental editor is a professional who knows when a story is working and when it is not. Developmental editors are literary experts with many years of experience as analytical readers of fiction. The sweetest part is that developmental editors know how to guide you in making your stories the best they can possibly be. When a manuscript is accepted by a traditional publishing house, the first editor that would be assigned to work with its author would be a D.E. This individual's job would be to help that author push their writing—to improve on it until it becomes good enough to be made into a novel destined to SELL and rack up very favorable reviews.

Do you want to guess which category of writers rarely use developmental editors? The ones that self-publish. Sadly, many in this group are not aware of this type of editing. As a result, there are thousands of badly written self-published novels out there. Lack of developmental editing is one of the reasons some continue to conclude that the word 'self-published' is synonymous with mediocrity. It is, of course, an unfair analogy since there have been several self-published novels that were so good, big publishing houses have snatched them up and contracted their authors. Two such novels are *The Martian* by Andy Weir and *Legally Blond* by Amanda Brown. Both became movies.

Should you work with a D.E., your manuscript turned into a novel, is likely to be assessed as a well-thought-out book and stands to receive favorable reviews. At this point, however, you may be thinking, 'But I already have a beta reader. Why should I work with whatever a developmental editor is? What's the big *difference?'* (**NOTE:** A beta reader may be someone—a friend or a neighbor—you'll probably ask to read your novel's manuscript and suggest improvements before you publish.)

KEY DIFFERENCES BETWEEN BETA READERS & DEVELOPMENTAL EDITORS

Some beta readers are not very reliable at being objective critics of manuscripts. Developmental editors are. A beta reader, at worst, might be that good friend or colleague who has only a limited understanding of what good writing is. A developmental editor, on the other hand, is an expert at analyzing manuscripts and guiding writers, through conferencing with them, to fix their work; the D.E. knows they must deliver for the editing fee charged. A beta reader can sometimes lose objectivity and guide you to write *their* story instead of helping you perfect *your* story. Not so with developmental editors. When you work with one, that D.E. will be helping you to tell *your* stories the best way *you* can. And then there are the beta readers who will return your manuscript with no changes recommended and a ton of praises for it. The D.E. you work with, however, will isolate the flaws in your story and send you notes that will help you to come up with fixes. Beginning writers, planning to self-publish, need to be wary of non-literary beta readers who may just be people who read bad books and love them. Mind you! I'm not saying a flat-out 'no' to beta readers, I'm just saying that when you rely *exclusively* on them, you place yourself on a slippery slope at the bottom of which, one-star reviews await.

INCULCATING THE MINDSET OF A D.E.

As a self-publishing novelist, you need to think like a one-person traditional publisher. You need to regard your manuscript as if it's one you have just accepted from someone else whose writing ability you're doubtful about. You must endeavor to put your own manuscript through a rigorous editing process as a traditional publisher would: Get it edited for development, get it copy-edited, and finally, get it proofread.

But since this conversation deals primarily with developmental editing, I'll take you on a tour of what happens to a manuscript in that specific department.

With your manuscript in the hands of a developmental editor, that individual looks at your beginning to see if it arrests and intrigues; the dramatic development in it would be examined as well as the pace of it. The D.E. reads to see, to hear, to taste, to smell, to feel the echoes of life in your fiction. After critically reading your work, that D.E. will provide you notes that will help you rethink and rewrite things to help you push your story to its most effective draft.

MY FIRST EXPERIENCE WORKING WITH A D.E.

After the manuscript of my first novel, *APATA: The Story of a Reluctant Criminal* was accepted by Heinemann Educational Books of London, my developmental editor read the manuscript and questioned things that gave him pause. There were times when he won me over on a point and caused me to either rewrite something or delete it altogether. A developmental editor will know when you are overwriting or underwriting at any point in your story. I recall being cautioned about a passage where I described a South American location in gushing, poetic prose as if from a John Steinbeck novel. 'Harold,' my D.E. wrote, *'it is obvious you love that location. Restrain yourself, however, with your description of it. It's too much!'* There was also another point in my novel where I warned, at length, that policemen are in danger of being contaminated by the evil they battle. 'Harold, he wrote, *'don't distract yourself and readers with metaphysical discourses and in the process, lose the thread of your story.'*

My D.E. made critical comments and asked questions. Through his input, I was able to fine-tune aspects of the plot, character-motivation, settings, descriptions, etc. He kept me on my toes, and honest about myself and the story I was telling. Through our interactions, my manuscript became the best it could have been. It was a bitter-sweet experience—at times more bitter than sweet. I persevered, however, and in the end, I became a better writer and an avid believer in the developmental-editing process.

Every writer who is serious about their manuscript NEEDS to work with a *developmental editor*. William Maxwell Perkins (20 September 1884 to 17 June 1947) was the developmental editor who discovered and guided the literary talents of Thomas Wolfe, F. Scott Fitzgerald, and Ernest Hemingway, among other writers. Wolfe wrote *Look Homeward Angel*; Fitzgerald wrote *The Great Gatsby*, and Hemingway wrote *For Whom the Bell Tolls*. (I'm sure you know the latter works. If not, get to know them. Why? When one reads critically acclaimed novels, one is exposed to effectively crafted fiction. This, in turn, rubs off on one. It *is* true that the more a writer reads the better a writer writes.)

THE REQUIRED MINDSET TO WORK WITH A D.E.

Good writers are always open to frank criticism. As writers, we need to be constantly mindful of our egos getting in the way of smooth relationships with developmental editors. Be aware: a D.E. will *never* tell you what to write to make anything in your manuscript better. *You* are the writer! Your D.E. will express a reservation about something. If you agree with them, you fix it; if you disagree, the astute developmental editor will give you the benefit of the doubt. As a writer, you will need to see your developmental editor as a mind-partner—that person who will be pushing you to see possibilities unthought-of in your own story. Good developmental editors help nudge writers to enhance their stories. Developmental editors also help at those times when something isn't working but we don't know exactly why.

All fiction manuscripts benefit from developmental editing. The first-time fiction writer needs to see fiction writing in the same vein as filmmaking: a collaborative art. Make your fiction writing a joint creative project by working with a developmental editor; it does not take anything away from you since, as I said, a developmental editor NEVER tells you what to write. They might tell you where something needs to be stronger and leave you to add that strength. They might tell you that Character 'A' is not believable, why they feel that way, and leave you to imbue that character with authenticity.

SO, HOW MIGHT YOU FIND DEVELOPMENTAL EDITING FOR FREE?

Is there a college or university in your town/city that runs fiction writing classes? If so, the literary professional running those classes can be someone you can approach to be your developmental editor. If that college or university has a fiction writing program, you might consider approaching staffers in that faculty who teach it. Maybe there's a writer in residence that you might be able to approach to be your developmental editor. Why not? Nothing ventured, nothing gained. Between a college and a university, you may be able to find a literary professional directly involved in fiction writing who might agree to be your D.E. Also, if you are a self-publishing writer in a community of experienced writers **who were traditionally published***, consider approaching one of them. Ask them if they would agree to help you by being your developmental editor. Yes, most writers can be busy with their own work, but you may be able to find one who won't mind being a mentor of sorts to you. I have helped and continue to help many first-time fiction writers who have approached me, despite laboring over my own literary projects. I enjoy helping beginning fiction writers. I'm sure that there are many others like me.

*Fiction writers whose books were published by traditional publishers know how rigorous the process of working with developmental editors is. They also know that in the grueling process of developmental editing, there's no crying in fiction writing.

MAKE SURE YOU HAVE A TIGHT SYNOPSIS OF YOUR MANUSCRIPT BEFORE PITCHING FOR A D.E.

Here's the reason: Someone who may consider helping you, will want to know what your novel is about before making a commitment. So, how do you provide this information? Will you launch into a monologue that outlines your book? Who has the time to listen to you rambling on about what your 300-page novel is about? Should you hand them your hefty manuscript and expect them to read it? Neither. What you do is give that individual a two-page synopsis. The big question to you at this point is, do you know how to write one? If the answer is no, go to your browser, type in the keywords, '**Synopsis writing Jericho.**' A lot of information on synopsis writing and more will show up. You'll be walked through it.

WHAT MIGHT YOU SAY TO A DEVELOPMENTAL EDITOR?

So, you've found a literary professional at a college or a university; or you found a writer who was traditionally published who agrees (after reading your synopsis) to assess your manuscript objectively and critically with the intent to help you make it better. What do you say to that person—in terms of what it is exactly you're asking them to do? Try the following or something like it: *"I'm asking you to read my manuscript critically and objectively. I will be open to everything that you have problems with once it helps me to have a better story in the end. If something in my plot doesn't add up or make sense, tell me. If something about a character bothers you, tell me. If you feel I need to research deeper into some detail or into some procedure in my manuscript, let me know. I will be open-minded and respectful of your feedback because I am matured, and my goal is to put out a solid manuscript with your help."* Something like that.

HOW DO YOU REWARD SOMEONE HELPING OUT AS YOUR DEVELOPMENTAL EDITOR?

Be honest up-front about your ability or inability to pay for their help. If you are cash-strapped, let that individual know that their name will be in your book's acknowledgments. Also, let your D.E. know that they are at the head of the line for a free, autographed copy if it comes out in paperback; or a free eBook or PDF if it is published digitally only.

EASING INTO THE RELATIONSHIP WITH A D.E.

After a literary professional agrees to look at the synopsis of your novel, tell that individual you can either provide a print-out of it or if they prefer, you can email it to them. If the person agrees to you emailing your synopsis, ask if an attachment would be preferred or the actual synopsis embedded in the body of the email. (I find that embedding the synopsis in the body of the email is better since it allows the recipient to read the synopsis directly from their handheld device if they do not have the software to do a download.)

If after that literary professional reads your synopsis, they ask for your manuscript, your relationship with a developmental editor begins.

BUT WHAT IF YOU CANNOT FIND A LITERARY PROFESSIONAL AT AN ACADEMIC INSTITUTION OR LOCATE A TRADITIONALLY PUBLISHED WRITER WHO MIGHT HELP?

Then you would have no other alternative but to pay an editorial service. There are companies that offer developmental editing; just seek them out.

HOW TO PROOFREAD YOUR WORK BEFORE SENDING IT OFF TO A D.E.

The first step will be to create some distance between yourself and your writing. The reason for this is to enable you to see it somewhat objectively and spot typos and omissions you couldn't isolate because you have been too close to your work. Many writers who self-publish believe they can proofread their manuscripts; it is a fallacy, however. Writers cannot do it *effectively*. This is because they are too close to what they have written.

An interesting disconnect takes place between what is *in* our minds against what is *on* the paper or screen when we read over what we have written. Let me illustrate: The following sentence pops into my head: **'MY LIFE IS A SERIES OF RECURRING MOMENTS OF ANXIETY.'** I feel it is a great line that I need to get down; so, in the eagerness of the moment I write: **'MY LIFE IS SERIES OF RECURRING MOMENTS OF ANXIETY.'** And every time I re-read the latter sentence on paper or from a screen, I only read what's in my head where there's an 'A' before the word 'series' even though it's missing on the screen or that printed sheet. And that's why we all need objective proofreaders before our work is deemed ready to be typeset.

But let's not get so far ahead; let's get back to our raw manuscripts: We do not want to send them riddled with typos to our developmental editors. We, therefore, need to find ways to catch and correct as many mistakes in our manuscripts as we could. The following are a few methods writers employ to proofread their own work:

a: PUT YOUR MANUSCRIPT IN *COLD STORAGE*

Put it away for a month or more and start working on something else. What you're trying to do is to create that personal distance between yourself and your story. After revisiting it, you may find that you're discovering typos, omissions, and other mistakes.

b: REFORMAT, PRINT OUT, READ

Somehow the perspective can feel as if you're reading a printed book. Something about a print-out helps to catch flaws. You might even take it a step further: Justify a chapter of your manuscript; make it single-spaced and print it out. It will appear as if reading someone else's work and help you see typos and omissions. Do this for each chapter.

(A popular variation of the above is to read what you've written aloud.)

c: EMAIL CHAPTER AFTER CHAPTER TO YOURSELF

Copy and then paste one single-spaced chapter after another *into* the body of an email to yourself. Change the font to 12-point, Times New Roman. Send it off, and then read it on your smartphone. I don't know if it's because of the size of the screen or that it looks like someone else's eBook, but a somewhat objective distance will be achieved between you and what you read on your phone's screen.

d: USE THE TEXT-TO-SPEECH (TTS) FEATURE ON YOUR PC OR MAC AND LISTEN TO YOUR WORK READ-BACK TO YOU

By and by, you will HEAR the gaps that denote missing words and typos. As a bonus, you may also hear too-close repetitions, lumpy flow, and downright bad sentences. I swear by this method. I am, you see, someone who suffers from acute anxiety and would often miss typos in my work—never mind how often or how loudly I re-read passages. For me, the TTS feature in my Word program falls into the 'best-thing-since-sliced-bread' category.

FOR PC USERS: There is a Text-To-Speech feature built into Microsoft Word that you may not be aware of. It carries a capital 'A' aligned to a symbol of sound waves. The 'READ ALOUD' program allows you to sit back, close your eyes and listen to your manuscript. Should you hear something that's not right, you simply stop the playback, make a correction, and then continue from where the playback stopped. I swear by this feature. Type the following keywords into your browser, **'5 ways to make your windows computer speak to you'** and you will find a tutorial on how to access this feature in Microsoft Word.

FOR MAC USERS: Go to YouTube, type the following into the search field, **'How to set your mac to read to you'**, and you will find a video tutorial on how to use the TTS feature in the Apple system.

IN CONCLUSION

Believe me, it is unsettling to discover a lot of typographical errors in your manuscript after sending it off to someone to read. I recall the times I have sent out manuscripts to a colleague who publishes traditionally, only to discover, afterward, that there are blatant typos I should have spotted and rectified. What did I do on those occasions? I quickly sent follow-up emails that said, *'Scrap that manuscript I sent you earlier. I made some corrections in it. Will resend updated version!'* I can assure you; it's not a nice feeling when you must do that. The remedy is to make sure the manuscript you send out has been raked over for typos and omissions. It also helps to think as a copy editor as you write. Think like a developmental editor too—anticipate story weaknesses your D.E. might find and see if you can fix them. Write defensively.

CONVO #2:

5 Things You Need to Take into Consideration *Before* Sending Your Manuscript to a D.E.

In the following convo, I'll be sharing five 'considerations' you must be aware of before sending your manuscript to a D.E. I'll be dissecting forced plots. I'll be detailing the importance of characters in your work having backstories. I will speak on how to imbue your own multifaceted personality into the characters you create, and in so doing make them real. I'll impress upon you the dangers of ineptly constructed sentences and how they can turn readers away from your writing. In the end, I will speak about the importance of doing in-depth research for your manuscript.

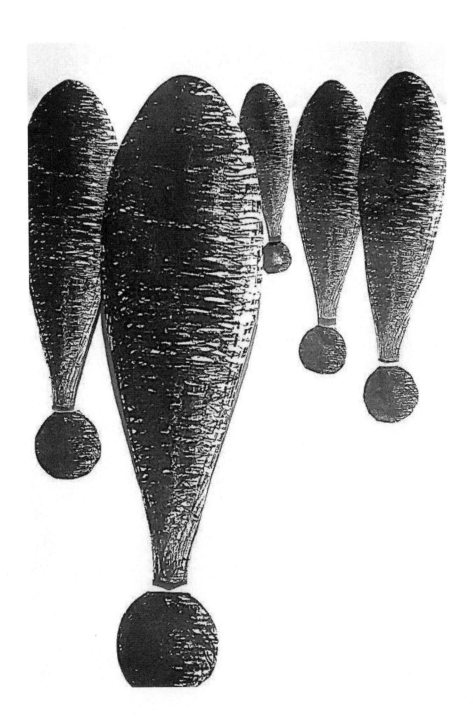

5 THINGS YOU NEED TO TAKE INTO CONSIDERATION *BEFORE* SENDING YOUR MANUSCRIPT TO A D.E.

But before we get to them, prime yourself for what's to come by asking yourself two questions: *Is my plot well thought-out? Are my characters real and feel as if they breathe?* Let's consider the last question. So, how can a writer ensure that his characters breathe—that they come over to a reader as real? I'll tell you how *I* make that happen and hope it may work for you also.

I imbue all my characters with a range of emotional values that I possess or with the expressed emotional values of individuals I have studied. I, however, always begin with myself. I examine 'me' as the human animal I am. I fill my unkind characters with the unkindness I can dredge up from within. I infuse my good characters with my inherent goodness. In short, I draw from the Yin and Yang of my personality to create the hearts of both protagonists and antagonists—the good, the bad, the ugly, and the indifferent. As such, I whisper to myself a lot: "What would you do in a situation like this, Harold?" ... "You are in this situation right now! How are you feeling deep inside?" ... "What are you thinking and what would you say, Harold?" I lend realism to my characters by living through them. I pour myself into them; I pour others that I know or have studied into them, too.

But let's get to the 5 considerations, shall we?

CONSIDERATION #1:

FORCED AND UNFORCED PLOTS:

Some first-time writers have the tendency to control their plots too tightly. They make them follow predetermined courses to predetermined climaxes. There are many times, however, when characters in a plot cry out to go somewhere else. That's when writers ought to listen and take heed. When they do not, they end with forced, implausible plots. Let's take a deeper look at this.

AN ANALYSIS OF A FORCED PLOT

Let me create an example: An inexperienced writer sets out to write a short story about a nineteen-year-old named Claire who is an ex-stripper, ex-prostitute, recovering drug addict, and the mother of four fatherless children in the social system. Claire also has a dangerous ex-lover (the father of one of her children) who is soon to be released from prison for stalking and abusing her physically. This writer, however, is fixated on writing a redemption story in which Claire finds Jesus, falls in love with a young preacher, marries him, and together they live happily ever after. It is the story this writer is *insistent* on telling the way *they* want to tell it and in so doing, touch readers deeply. But what this writer does not take into consideration is the 'backstory' he created for Claire—that it would never lead comfortably to where he intends the story to end. ('Backstory' is all about the history or background a writer creates for a fictional character.)

But let's look at the plot outline the writer in question has created for his redemption story:

One night, Claire hears singing from a little church on her block. She enters and sits at the back of the pews. The handsome, young preacher captivates her. Eventually, he does an altar call for new souls. She goes up. He spots Claire. They look at one another and it's love at first sight. He prays for her and she accepts Christ. He asks her to hang around and then they talk. She tells him every sordid thing about herself—about her past, her children, about the imprisoned father of one of them who would soon be out—about how dangerous he is. She tells him everything. He tells her that he understands and that God would make her whole and the love they feel for each other would make them complete. He takes her home to his parents— a retired police officer and an ex-social worker, respectively. He tells them about her life and that he would be marrying her within a couple of months. They are never happier. They accept Claire into the family and give the young couple their blessings. The young preacher marries Claire, and they live happily ever after.

The above is the perfect definition of a FORCED PLOT—one the inexperienced writer wants to unfold exactly the way they need it to despite the realities of the characters' backstories that scream, "Won't work!" Why? The answer is simple: If the character of Claire is written as real, that happily-ever-after ending would be near impossible. Claire would be aware of the weight of the conflicts surrounding her life. If she truly loves the young preacher, she is likely to deter him from getting serious with her. She might shy away from accompanying him to meet his parents.

Now, to the young pastor: He, on hearing about her past and her current challenges, *would* have sympathy for her tragic life. He's a man of God, after all, and would have compassion. However, he would be extremely cautious about having a love-relationship with such a woman and quickly making her his wife. He may decide to get her the rehabilitative help she needs, instead.

And then there are his parents. Can we see a mother who was a social worker with years of experience dealing with recovering and relapsing female drug addicts—some who were prostitutes scarred with domestic abuse—encouraging her son to have anything to do with a woman such as Claire? And then there's the young preacher's father, an ex-policeman who, like his wife, would be equally wary about his son's tainted choice. The mere fact that Claire is a social mess is the catalyst to move the story in another direction that may turn out to be more riveting.

I hope the above analysis gives you a stronger handle on how to evaluate the plot-outline of your novel before submitting it to a developmental editor.

CONSIDERATION #2:

YOUR CHARACTERS' BACKSTORIES:

In the above example, we see how a story can suffer if its writer forces its characters to take predetermined routes instead of allowing the backstory of each character to determine their individual paths. In the following example you will see the opposite of the above: when a fiction writer starts out with a central character for whom no backstory has been established:

Let's imagine I'm writing a novel in which MIKE, my protagonist, is introduced as an amiable plumber and stable family man. His only vice is playing poker in his garage with his retired neighbor ERIC. At some point, well into the story, I create a scene in which Mike loses a game to Eric, but instead of laughing it off, as he and Eric normally would, Mike flies into a rage, pulls an automatic pistol, shoots Eric in the face, calmly dismembers the body, dumps it in the local landfill, and then returns to clean up the crime scene.

How do you think the above scene might strike a developmental editor? Chances are, I would be sent a critical note saying, *I have a problem with Mike. In no part of the manuscript prior to him abruptly killing Eric, have you shown him to be a dangerous man with a murderous temper. Further, in no chapter prior to this, have you established that Mike owns a pistol or knows how to use one. You need to fix a few things. To do so, I'm recommending that you give him a backstory of some sort that tells he is comfortable around guns, owns one, and that he has the capacity to be a murderer. What about something like this: Make Mike an ex-marine with a past he doesn't talk about. Create a flashback scene, maybe in the early part of the book, showing him back in Afghanistan and coldly shooting a captured Taliban fighter in the face. Something like that. You're the writer. I'm sure you can work it out.*

CONSIDERATION #3:

ARE YOU INVESTED IN YOUR CHARACTERS OR ARE THEY MERE PUPPETS?

Let us assume that in a plot you've written, there's a character named JANICE who must drive into a gas station (attached to a 7-Eleven outlet), get some gas, and then proceed to pick up her daughter from ballet practice. If, in the latter progression, there are to be no deviations, the character Janice becomes your puppet: You the writer have chosen to stand above her, pull her strings, to make her do *exactly* what *you* want. The scene, therefore, can go like this:

> *Janice pulls into the gas station with the 7-Eleven attached. She's happy that it's midafternoon. There are many vacant pumps. She pulls into one and turns off her car's engine. She climbs out and starts filling the tank of the aging Toyota Camry. By the time she arrives at Casey's ballet class, it would be over.*
>
> *The pump clicks. She gives it a few squeezes for good measure, hangs the hose up, closes the gas cap to her car, and pulls out to pick up Casey.*

But what if you, the writer, crawl *into* your character, become Janice—and as yourself—recall the last time you visited a gas station, and let Janice see some of the things and experience some of the things *you* would. Let's see:

> *You pull into the gas station with the 7-Eleven attached. You're happy that it's midafternoon. There are vacant pumps. You pull into one and turn off your car's engine. You climb out and start filling the tank of your aging Toyota Camry. You think of your daughter, Casey: By the time you arrive at her ballet class, it would be over.*
>
> *As your tank fills, you look around. You find yourself gazing off to the entrance of the 7-Eleven. You see a woman leaving while eating a slice of pizza. Your stomach grumbles. You realize that you haven't eaten since that morning. The pump*

clicks. You give it a few squeezes for good measure, hang the hose up, and close the gas cap. You lock the driver's door and start for the entrance of the store.

You enter; the smell of pepperoni stirs your taste buds. You look around. You join the very short line to the cashier. Your eyes fall on the seven-hundred-million-dollar lottery sign next to the cash register. You get up to the counter, buy a cheeseburger, a soda, and like an afterthought, a lottery ticket.

"Reminds me ... I need to get one of those," says an elderly female voice behind you. "You don't have a ticket, you don't have a chance!" Soon after, the voice mumbles regretfully, "Damn! I only have enough cash to buy me a soda!"

You are a very kind-hearted individual. You turn to the stranger and say, "I'll get one for you."

"Oh! Thank you! Thank you, Honey! You are an angel! Bless your soul!"

"Don't worry about it," you say, smiling.

"Let me take a picture of you, Honey."

"Okay."

Back in your car, you think of the elderly Black woman. What if she wins? Will she tell the story of the kind White woman who helped her buy the ticket?

You chuckle, key your car, and pull out to pick up Casey.

Now, let's do the following exercise. We'll take the above second person point-of-view references (**you**, **your**, etc.), and replace it with the third person point-of-view: **Janice**, **she**, etc. Let's see how your fiction deepens and comes alive:

Janice pulls into the gas station with the 7-Eleven attached. She's happy that it's midafternoon. There are many vacant pumps. She pulls into one and turns off her car's engine. She climbs out and starts filling the tank of her aging Toyota Camry. By the time she arrives at Casey's ballet class, it would be over.

As the tank fills, she looks around. She finds herself gazing off to the entrance of the 7-Eleven. An obese woman exits while eating a slice of pizza. Janice's stomach gurgles. She realizes that she hasn't eaten since that morning. The pump clicks. She *gives it a few squeezes for good measure then hangs the hose up. She closes the gas cap, locks the driver's door and starts for the entrance of the store.*

She enters to the pervasive smell of pepperoni and looks around. She joins the very short line to the cashier. Janice's eyes fall on the seven-hundred-million-dollar lottery sign next to the cash register. At the counter, she buys a cheeseburger, a soda, and like an afterthought, a lottery ticket.

"Reminds me. ... I need to get one of those," says an elderly female voice behind her. "You don't have a ticket, you don't have a chance!" Soon after, the voice mumbles regretfully, "Damn ... I only have enough cash on me to buy a soda!"

Janice turns to the stranger. "Don't worry, I'll get one for you."

"Oh! Thank you! Thank you, Honey! You're an angel! Bless your heart!"

"Don't worry about it," Janice says, smiling.

"Let me take a picture of you, Honey."

"Okay."

Back in her car, she thinks of the elderly Black woman. What if she wins? Will she tell the story of the kind White woman who helped her buy the ticket?

Janice chuckles, keys her car and pulls out to pick up Casey.

Immerse yourself into your characters. Immerse real people you know into them. The latter works for realism. Never treat your characters as mere puppets. Instead, possess and breathe consciousness into them.

Here is a further example of what I mean: As I work on this manuscript, I look out the glass door to my backyard. I see the rails of the uncovered deck under the overcast sky. I think of the summer afternoon I saw a pair of birds—brown thrashers, nestled together on a section of the rails. I also think of the two dogs that would bark rabidly at me from next door whenever I went onto my own deck. Now, If I were to write about someone going out there, I won't stand outside that 'someone' and write:

Andy walked out the glass door and onto his deck. He looked down at the RC car track he had made in his backyard.

Instead, I would invest 'Andy' with my experiences and write:

Andy started for the back deck. As he approached the glass door that led out to it, he saw a pair of plump brown thrashers nestled together on a handrail. Husband and wife? They looked so intimate. He hesitated and thought he should let them have their moment. Maybe they were tired of flying. A few minutes after, they both stood. Did they sense him watching them? He heard a peal of laughter from the front lawn and turned away. His boys were playing with the water hose. When he turned back to the scene out the glass door, the brown thrashers were gone.

He walked onto the deck and immediately the neighbor's dogs began barking wildly at him. He ignored them and gazed at the RC car track he had made in his backyard.

CONSIDERATION #4:

YOUR SENTENCES:

Success at the writer's craft comes down to how good *each* of your sentences is. I once read a self-published novel with the following sentence: *"Oh, my God!" Amanda bellowed loudly through clenched teeth. ...'* It was a head-scratching sentence. I thought, *How the hell can someone bellow loudly through clenched teeth. To bellow loudly one needs to open one's mouth widely; as such, the teeth won't be clenched.* And after a series of questionable sentences, I laid the novel aside. Subsequently, I met the young novelist at a 'Meetup' for new authors where I was a guest. I took her aside. "I'm sorry, but your novel is really bad," I said gently.

"I know," she said. Her voice was low.

"Then why did you put it out there?"

"This guy who started his own publishing company told me it was good—but I always had doubts about the manuscript. I always wanted to find a writer's coach or somebody like that to help me."

"That would have definitely helped."

I lost touch with her.

Back to the discussion: Can you imagine how your developmental editor would think of you, after finding a sentence like the above in your manuscript? Try not to saddle your D.E. with serious sentence issues; such falls under the domain of the copy editor who will be reading your manuscript for syntax, spelling, etc. Your developmental editor will accept your manuscript with the understanding that every writer encounters minor issues with the basics of grammar and punctuation. Primarily, your D.E. will be reading for the story—to help you convert your manuscript into an engrossing novel.

CONSIDERATION # 5:

HOW MUCH RESEARCH HAS GONE INTO YOUR MANUSCRIPT?

Background research for your manuscript is of utmost importance. Let us suppose you decide to write a short story entitled 'COCKPIT: One Day in the Life of An Airline Captain.' But you've never seen an airline pilot's workspace. Should that fact stop you from penning such a story? No. You're a writer; you do the research. You find YouTube videos that give you tours of inside an airliner's cockpit. You find interviews with airline captains. You then write your story. Chances are, one of your readers who may happen to be an airline pilot is likely to murmur, "Hmmm... I bet this writer is a pilot or was a pilot."

At the beginning of our careers as writers, most of us have been told, 'Write what you know.' Serious writers, however, have modified that adage to, 'Research to know, and then write from that new knowledge-base.'

Be sure the details in your manuscript are researched painstakingly before you submit your work. Speaking about this takes me back to the time I was doing research for my first novel based on a manhunt for a fugitive in Guyana, South America. Back then there wasn't the Internet to find stuff easily. I took trips to the Guyana National Archives in Georgetown, Guyana, South America, to dig up old newspapers, take notes and do sketches. I was there almost daily—as if I worked there. (I can still see Mr. Tommy Payne the archivist chuckling as he looked at me before saying, "What are you doing, Mr. Bascom? Why are you researching an old criminal?")

Today, however, online archives are literally at our fingertips. Despite this, there are many first-time writers, eager to make passive income, who turn out under-researched manuscripts that become published novels, novels that could have been saved had the time been taken to do the relevant research to support their plots.

I reviewed a highly promoted novel in which a medical device, being beta-tested, tells its wearers when each is going to die and turns most of them into killers for reprisal or revenge. To ensure that I was reviewing a medical drama from an informed position, I did online-research into how clinical tests are to be conducted by FDA guidelines and found that within the book, procedures and progressions were all wrong—implausible. In my review, I wrote: *"So, let us look at such a clinical test in real life. Volunteers may have had reservations/objections to the watch based on concerns that are either religious, cultural, or ethical. As such, it might have been interesting to have more scenes showing how the volunteers reacted initially. The author, however, just leaves the reader to believe that each of the volunteers, after being told that the device heralds impending death, got excited and said, "It's going to tell me as bluntly as that—that I'm going to die? —Oh, goody! Yes! Wonderful! Sign me up!"*

Had this self-publishing author worked with a developmental editor, he would have been guided to do much more research for his manuscript. He would have been warned that his lack of in-depth investigation into the testing of new medical devices stood to make his entire story teeter and collapse. Had he worked with a developmental editor, his novel might have garnered a genuine four or five-star review from me, instead of the single star I gave it.

BONUS BIT:

If by now, you feel your story is tight, and you have completed your synopsis. It is time to send out your manuscript to your chosen developmental editor. Before you do, however, make sure it is properly formatted. The following guidelines will work. It is standard:

- Use a 1-inch margin on all sides.
- Use a title page that carries only the name of your novel, your by-line, your address and contact information.
- Don't number the title page. Begin numbering with the first page of the text of the book, usually the introduction, prologue, or chapter one.
- Use a header on each page, including your name, the title of your novel in all caps, and the page number.
- Start each new chapter on its own page, one-third of the way down the page.
- The chapter number and chapter title should be in all caps, separated by two hyphens: CHAPTER 1--THE HARE.
- Begin the body of the chapter, four to six lines below the chapter title.
- Indent fives spaces for each new paragraph.
- Double-space the entire text.
- Use a standard font, 12-point type. Times New Roman, Arial, or Courier.
- Use 20-lb. bond paper.

At this point, I say, *Best of luck finding a developmental editor you can work with!* Who knows? I may come across your book and review it.

CONVO #3:

How to Prevent Your Novel from Possibly Being Tossed Because of One Inappropriate Word in It

Phrases and sentences form the backbone of our work as writers. Mastering our word-use, therefore, becomes integral to our self-respect as wordsmiths. Words express our tone and our style and give notice of our range. As a self-publishing writer, you need to be acutely aware of every word that you use and to rely on the editing process as a safety net for whatever you produce as a writer.

In this conversation, I'll start by griping about a single sentence I came across in a new writer's novel—a sentence that had one inappropriate word that caused me to lay the book aside. I'll go on to list the negative things that single word revealed about the writer. I will then follow with an urging, that new writers own up to the serious responsibility of moving hell and heaven to get their manuscripts properly edited by either a professional human editor, an editing program, or a combination of both. This convo ends with a few helpful links to editing programs and another to the Fiverr website where inexpensive editors can be contracted.

Janice Tapper pulls into the gas station with the 7-Eleven convenience store attached. She arrives readily to a vacant pump. She switches off the engine of her aging Toyota Camry, gets out, and begins filling the tank for the rest of the week. *By the time I arrive at Ct- allet class, it should be over.* The insistent sound of a jackhammer or something ma— er look toward the h'ghway running past. Over it, a sprawling commercial comp— thing shape. It's going to be a craft store. She has researched the company's website. as applied for a position there. She contemplates leaving her job as a waitress bec— f her daughter Casey who's no ____. She thinks of 'Miss Glenda' stired African American librar_____ he apartment immediately be nd kept Casey until Janice got ho___ _at Glenda has been evicted. Jan nds it worrisome that when she's at work, her daughter is home alone until after ele m. Janice needs to find a job that would give her the choice of an early shift. That w he'd be home soon after her daughter gets in from school. She finds herself think again of 'Miss Glenda', the soft-spoken woman _ho used to work at the local commun ollege. After the apartment complex was b_____ the new management ha ympathetic with senior tenants who were fir__ __ie ends meet. There w _ few times Janice loaned 'Miss Glenda' mo___ ___ing over her head. hen the new owners raised the rent, Ke___ ___ant became extrem ficult for her and she was evicted. Whe__ ___he pump clicks, Jar as the handle a few squeezes for an e___ ___up the hose and cl ar's gas cap, she gets back in the c___ ___ou shouldn't do me Craig!' someone chortles. Janice ___ ___of the 7-Eleven. An ol is leaving as she eats a slice ___h growls. She realizes aten since this morning. She ___dbag, gets out, and—w rs—locks the door behind ___ediate aroma of peppe around at the shelves o' ___ll on the one-point-six-bill ns the very short line ___er, she buys a cheeseburge ign next to the c ___minds me! I need to get on the an aftertl ___fully, 'Damn! I only have enc elderly for ___u don't have a ticket, you d , after, ___African American woman. "D t so ___you. Honey? You're an ang— ____illing. The woman taber— Hey," Janice free-___ ___lar

HOW TO PREVENT YOUR NOVEL FROM POSSIBLY BEING TOSSED BECAUSE OF ONE INAPPROPRIATE WORD IN IT

After the manuscript of my first novel was accepted by London's Heinemann Educational Books, I had a run-in with my copy editor over an inappropriate word I had used in a sentence. I cannot remember the word exactly, so I'll represent it with 'X.'. My copy editor, however, was very condescending about it. What I cannot forget, however, was the disdain and mockery inherent in the note he sent me:

'The word 'X' doesn't fit what you're hoping to express. You can, however, use 'P', 'Q' R' or 'S.' Take your pick.'

It angered me, but I took my pick and my novel was better off because of it. I still feel bad about the subtle insult though it happened, to date, over thirty-one years ago. But it was good for me: It made me acutely conscious that a writer needs to find that appropriate word within any given context within their narrative.

As such, I have grown to be the kind of literary coach who pushes new writers to always work hard to find that appropriate word, since the wrong one carries negative connotations for the writer. It reveals much. In my need to impress upon new crafters of literature the importance of the right word, I have penned this 'conversation' based on one fledgling writer's use of a single inappropriate word in the following descriptive sentence:

'It was a very dark Southern night. Eyes of wild animals gleamed from the dark bushes off the sides of the narrow country road, and crickets squeaked here and there.'

The above sentence came from a self-published paperback mailed to me by a young woman hoping for an honest review. It had some heft—over four hundred printed pages, which signaled how much hard writing she had done. I settled in, began to read, came across the above sentence, and stopped. I couldn't continue. The sentence told me that it was not going to be worth my time. Ineptly crafted fiction leaves a bad taste in my mind. I did get back to the author, however. I wrote her a long letter on the importance of the appropriate word, which I hope was helpful to her.

As writers, we must strive to become wordsmiths—hammering away at our words and our sentences until each word is appropriate to what we intend to express. So, in this conversation, we'll toss the above sentence onto the anvil and beat on it. Firstly, let's see what it reveals about its author:

It tells that the author has a weak vocabulary. A writer who does not know that mice *squeak* and crickets *chirp*, will find it difficult to refute the weak-vocab conclusion. In the literary world, that single misused word easily invites disrespect to you as a writer. So, let's speak of what might cause a first-time writer to have a weak vocabulary. The answer is simple: not having read enough. To be a good fiction writer one must be a voracious reader of fiction and non-fiction in all kinds of genres and of varied subjects.

The broader we read, the more words we come across, which in turn expand our mental dictionaries. The writer who is aware that they need to improve on their vocabulary will also relish word games of every sort and subscribe to word-of-the-day apps—things like that. In the course of reading habitually, a new writer's vocabulary flourishes. What are the chances a well-read writer will not know the sounds made by different life forms? It will be highly unlikely.

Regarding me abandoning the above-referenced novel, one might say, *"Jeeze! You could have cut her some slack after she had written a four-hundred-page novel. How could her vocabulary be weak after writing such a long book? The misused* word could have been a typo, for Chri'sakes!" It could have been. That, however, tells us something else about the writer:

It says that the author failed to have her manuscript objectively edited or that she edited it herself. I doubt it was a case that the author did not know every manuscript needs editing before it is prepared for printing or final uploading. It is part of the creative writing process.

There are, however, throngs of new, self-publishing writers who do not care to be lectured about 'the creative writing process.' "Sheesh! What's that? Who cares?" This breed of writers believes creative writing is easy—a quick hustle from which impressive passive income stands to be made on Amazon KDP and other eBook publication platforms.

What is the root cause of the latter belief? One culprit is *YouTube* and the tons of videos that continually promote how easy books are to write. I came across a video in which a presenter promoted a dictaphone-type program that would enable a writer to easily 'talk' a manuscript into existence. I was compelled to speak out and commented thus:

'I've been a writer for thirty-plus years. With that experience, I KNOW that dictating is dictating, and writing is writing. I'm hard-pressed to grasp how someone can dictate a proper manuscript. The craft of writing involves the constant ordering and reordering of words to form active and passive sentences—the constant rewriting and rewriting of paragraphs. I doubt that (name of program withheld) will help someone produce a well-written manuscript by talking it into being. I may be vilified as an old out-of-touch writer-type, but for me, writing is writing—either by longhand or keyboard, and there are no shortcuts to that.'

Many disagreed, passionately.

But let's get back to the sentence that influenced this piece: The author of it confessed that she couldn't afford professional editing which can cost as much as $5000 to have the manuscript of a full novel edited. Self-publishing comes with a cost. As such, a writer from a low economic bracket may confront financial dilemmas on the road to publication. Should a struggling writer use hard-earned money to have a manuscript professionally edited, or should that money be reserved for food, clothes, and rent? The latter choice, invariably, wins out—especially if there are children in the mix. So, what does that writer do? The easiest course is to opt for self-editing or choose to have it peer-edited. The best option will be to seek to have it edited for free by someone in the fiction writing faculty of an academic institution. (CONVO #1 covers this, in depth.) Bottom-line: The need for quality editing is a serious requirement when self-publishing.

Another factor that prevents many self-publishing writers from producing good novels, is their reluctance to submit raw manuscripts for editing by other people. A writer in this category often feels that writing is 'personal'—an ego-driven one-man show. The truth is, it is not. Fiction writing is a collaborative art form just as filmmaking, in which one does not do it all. In moviemaking, there's the screenwriter, the director, the director of photography, the editor and in the background a creeping list of supporting talents. In self-publishing, likewise, there must be a writer (most likely, you), editors (other people—comprising of a developmental editor, a copy editor, and a proofreader), and finally the publisher, yourself.

Most writers who self-publish, however, make the effort to get their work edited but seek it only from their peers, which can prove problematic. (I elaborated on this in CONVO #1 under the section that looks at 'Beta Readers' vs. Developmental Editors.') What happens if someone new to the craft of writing gives their manuscript to a friend, who's not well read, to read critically? What happens if a new self-publishing writer with an underdeveloped vocabulary asks a peer whose vocabulary is equally underdeveloped to edit their work? What can result are sentences like the one under discussion.

SO, WHAT CAN A SELF-PUBLISHING WRITER WHO MIGHT NOT HAVE A BUDGET FOR 'FOUR-FIGURE PROFESSIONAL EDITING' DO?

#1: Seek it from a literary professional at your local college or university. (I discussed this in depth in CONVO #1.) Nothing will beat a live professional editor helping you out. If, however, the latter is not open to you, then the following may have to suffice:

#2: Find an editing tool/program that can be downloaded onto your computer. Use it to do the final editing of your manuscript for a mere fraction of the cost you'd pay to a professional editor or an editing service. There is a 'NY BOOK EDITORS' article on a variety of inexpensive editing tools. To find it type the following keywords into your browser: **'Instantly improve your writing with these 11 editing tools.'**

#3: Use the Fiverr website where professional editing can be found for an extremely small fee which can start as low as five dollars and going up to a few hundred dollars. The URL follows. Just type it into your browser:

www.fiverr.com

There is nothing more disconcerting to a novelist as reading their published work at a function and discovering typos, omissions, and bad sentences. I can speak to the latter experience. It's not easy to forget.

ENDING CAUTION: On a base level most of these editing tools (in their 'free' configurations), employ algorithms to catch only basic typographical mistakes. If you are a writer who has more than a basic grasp of grammar, there will be times when you will choose to ignore correction suggestions from any one or more of the above editing tools. They are, however, better than no editing at all.

CONVO #4

An Introduction to Choosing Points of View and How Tenses affect Them

Let's imagine that as a beginning writer, you're ready to hand your first story to someone to read, but before you do, that person says, "From what point of view is your story written?"

The question throws you. But don't panic. Smile and glance at your story's beginning; the clue to whatever point of view is there: If it starts something like: **'My name is Johnny Wells. I'm an army brat; I was born on a military base in Germany.'** *You can answer, "It's written in the first-person singular point of view."*

If it begins thus: **'Johnny Wells was an army brat; he was born on a military base in Germany.'** *You can answer, "It's written in the third-person point of view."*

You may be thinking, So, if there's a first-person and a third-person—what about the second-person?

That's why I feel you'll enjoy the following conversation. In it, I will explain what the first-person, singular; the second, and third-person points of view are. I will also show how the tense you use with each of the latter Points of View, affects your readers. (I will also touch lightly on 'how to show the thoughts of characters.')

At the end of this conversation, you will be able to use fundamental points of view and tenses, as tools to tell your stories the way you need to.

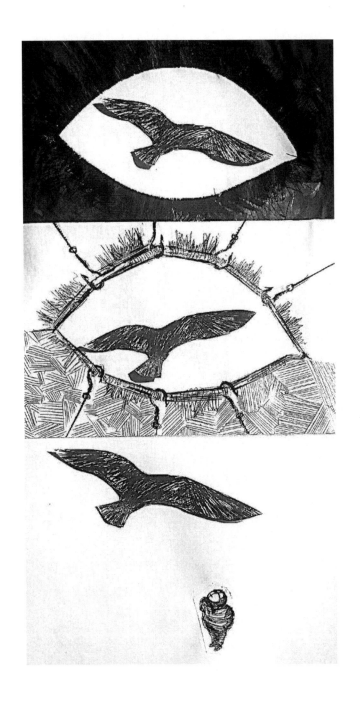

AN INTRODUCTION TO CHOOSING POINTS OF VIEW AND HOW TENSES AFFECT THEM

THE FIRST-PERSON SINGULAR POINT OF VIEW:

When someone writes a story in the FIRST-PERSON SINGULAR, it means the main character in a story will be telling it from the "I" Point Of View (POV). Everything will be seen through that 'I' person's eyes and every judgment will be made from that 'I' person's perception.

(**NOTE:** *There is also the FIRST-PERSON PLURAL voice in which stories are told from the "We" Point Of View—POV.)*

**EXAMPLE OF THE FIRST-PERSON SINGULAR VIEW
WRITTEN IN THE PAST TENSE:**

The annoying, beeping sound from my cell phone startled me awake. I reached out and shut it off. *God! I can't believe morning's here already!*
I tossed aside the comforter, heard gusting wind, and rain falling heavily. I sat up; eased my legs over the side of my bed. My left sock was missing.
The taint of something seeped into my bedroom. I must have fallen asleep after promising to put the trash in the garage.
I shuffled to the bathroom and looked at myself in the mirror. Didn't like those lines at the side of my lips; didn't like the darkness under my eyes. *I look like a raccoon. What's that spot on my neck? Was it there yesterday?*
"Mary Dean...you need to take care of yourself."
Is that the garbage truck I hear? —"Shit!" I grabbed a robe, slipped it on, and dashed into the kitchen. I yanked the bag of trash out of its receptacle and hurried for the garage.
As the door rumbled up, the morning chill stung my face. I ran to the side of the house where the wheeled bin was, tossed the kitchen trash in, and began hauling it, under the downpour, to the sidewalk.

The truck was just two houses away.

I made it and glanced at the vehicle. The driver seemed to be shaking his head at me. I guess I looked like a wet dog. *To hell with him!*

EXAMPLE OF THE FIRST-PERSON SINGULAR VIEW
WRITTEN IN THE PRESENT TENSE:

The annoying, beeping sound of my cell phone startles me awake. I reach out and shut it off. *God! I can't believe morning's here already!*

I toss aside the comforter, hear gusting wind, and rain, falling heavily. I sit up; ease my legs over the side of my bed. My left sock is missing.

The taint of something seeps into my bedroom. I must have fallen asleep after promising to put the trash in the garage.

I shuffle to the bathroom and look at myself in the mirror. Don't like those lines at the side of my lips; don't like the darkness under my eyes. *I look like a raccoon. What's that spot on my neck? Was it there yesterday?*

"Mary Dean...you need to take care of yourself."

Is that the garbage truck I hear? —"Shit!" I grab a robe, slip it on, and dash into the kitchen. I yank the bag of trash out of its receptacle and hurry for the garage.

As the door rumbles up, the morning chill stings my face. I run to the side of the house where the wheeled bin is, toss the kitchen trash in, and begin hauling the bin, under the downpour, to the sidewalk.

The truck is just two houses away.

I'm on time. I glance at the vehicle. The driver seems to be shaking his head at me. I probably look like a wet dog. *To hell with him!*

Before we continue to the second-person and third-person points of view, pause and consider tenses and how they affect points of view.

We'll also look at one way how a writer can show the thoughts of their characters:

TENSES:

When a story is written in the present tense it makes the reader feel as though they are riding along in real-time with whatever is happening in the narrative. When that same story is written in the past tense, however, the reader is being told about a ride that took place. As a writer, whatever tense you choose to tell a story in, is personal. (There are times when I would write one story in both tenses, as in the above examples, and then test the two versions on friends. The version with most 'likes' would be the final choice. But, then again, there are times when I know for sure that I must tell a story in a specific tense and nothing will shake me from that resolve. Again: It's always up to the writer.

SHOWING THE THOUGHTS OF CHARACTERS:

In the above excerpts, there are some lines in italics: *'God! I can't believe morning's here already!'*, *'I look like a raccoon. What's that spot on my neck? Was it there yesterday?'* and *'Is that the garbage truck I hear?'* Those are things Mary says in her mind—things that she thinks. So, when writers want to indicate thoughts of characters, they *can* be put in italics. NOTE: Thoughts are NOT enclosed in quotation marks; those are reserved for direct speech as in: "I look like a raccoon; what's that spot on my neck? Was it there yesterday?" Mary mumbled.

But let's continue with storytelling voices:

THE SECOND-PERSON POINT OF VIEW:

When someone writes a story in the SECOND PERSON, it means the writer will be referring to the main character in the story as 'you' and 'your'. It is also a purely passive voice that is not at all dynamic and arresting.

EXAMPLE OF THE SECOND-PERSON VIEW

WRITTEN IN THE PRESENT TENSE:

You are startled awake by the annoying, beeping sound from your cell phone. You reach out and shut it off. *God! You think. I can't believe morning's here already!*

You toss aside the comforter and hear gusting wind; rain falls heavily. You sit up; ease your legs over the side of your bed. Your left sock is missing.

The taint of something seeps into your bedroom. You must have fallen asleep after promising to put the trash in the garage.

You shuffle to the bathroom and look at yourself in the mirror. You do not like those lines at the side of your lips ... don't like the darkness under your eyes. You think you look like a raccoon. *What is that spot on your neck?* You think. *Was it there yesterday?*

"Mary Dean..." you mumble, "you need to take care of yourself."

You hear the garbage truck rumbling up the street. "Damn!" you swear. *The trash bin!* You haven't put it on the sidewalk. You grab a robe, slip it on, and dash into the kitchen. You yank the trash of out its receptacle and run for the garage.

As the door rumbles up, the morning chill stings your face. You dash out to the side of the house where the large, wheeled bin is, and toss the kitchen trash in. You drag the bin, under the downpour, to the sidewalk just in time.

You're sure the garbage truck's driver is shaking his head at you. You probably look like a wet dog. *To hell with him!* you think.

EXAMPLE OF THE SECOND-PERSON VIEW
WRITTEN IN THE PAST TENSE:

You were startled awake by the annoying, beeping sound from your cell phone. You reached out and shut it off. *God! You thought. I can't believe morning's here already!*

You tossed aside the comforter and heard the gusting wind; the rain fell heavily. You sat up; eased your legs over the side of your bed. Your left sock was missing.

The taint of something seeped into your bedroom. You most likely fell asleep after promising to put the trash in the garage.

You shuffled to the bathroom and looked at yourself in the mirror. You hated those lines at the side of your lips; didn't like the darkness under your eyes. You looked like a raccoon. *What is that spot on your neck?* You thought. *Was it there yesterday?*

"Mary Dean..." you mumbled, "you need to take care of yourself."

You heard the garbage truck rumbling up the street. "Damn!" you swore. *The trash bin!* You realized you didn't put it on the sidewalk. You grabbed a robe, slipped it on, and dashed into the kitchen. You yanked the trash of out its receptacle and hurry for the garage.

As the door rumbled up, the morning chill stung your face. You ran to the side of the house where the large, wheeled bin was and tossed the kitchen trash in. You dragged the bin, under the downpour, to the sidewalk just in time.

You were sure the garbage truck's driver was shaking his head at you. You probably looked like a wet dog. *To hell with him!* you thought.

I suspect we will agree that the second-person voice, or point of view—in past or present tense—is an awkward one to use in writing fiction. It is no wonder the second-person voice is not popular with writers. It is, however, the perfect voice of a film or stage director giving instructions to performers on a film-set or theatrical stage. If, for example, you have a director as a character in your novel who's instructing actors, the use of the second person POV will be fitting.

THE THIRD-PERSON POINT OF VIEW:

In the third person POV, the names of characters are used as well as pronouns like he, she, it, they, etc. This is the point of view from which most short stories and novels are written. This is so because the third-person point of view allows a writer to tell a story from multiple points of view; in short, more broadly.

In the following excerpts, you can tell what Mary sees and thinks; you can also show things she cannot know—like what Tony the garbage truck driver is thinking as he looks at her.

With the use of the third-person point of view, the writer can show the reader what Tony is thinking. The third-person point of view gives an author the all-seeing, all-knowing perspective of a God.

EXAMPLE OF THE THIRD-PERSON VIEW
IN THE PAST TENSE:

    Mary was startled awake by the beeping of her cell phone. She reached out and shut it off. *God!* she thought, *I can't believe morning's here already!*
    She tossed aside the comforter and heard gusting wind; the rain fell heavily. Mary Dean sat up; eased her legs over the side of her bed. Her left sock was missing.
    The taint of something seeped into her bedroom. she must have fallen asleep after promising to put the trash in the garage.
    She shuffled to the bathroom and looked at herself in the mirror. She didn't like those lines at the side of her lips; she didn't like the darkness under her eyes either. She thought she looked like a raccoon. *What's that spot on my neck? Was it there yesterday?*
    "Mary Dean...you need to take care of yourself."
    The garbage truck rumbled up the street. Mary heard it and swore. *The bin!* She hadn't put it on the sidewalk. She grabbed a robe, slipped it on, and dashed into the kitchen. She yanked the bag of trash out of its receptacle and hurried for the garage.
    As the door rumbled up, the morning chill stung her face. She ran to the side of the house where the large, wheeled bin was and tossed the kitchen trash in. She dragged the bin, under the downpour, to the sidewalk just in time.

    Tony, the garbage truck driver, just one house away, looked at Mary, drenched under the downpour. He shook his head. But he was glad she brought out her trash in time. *Hadn't* she *a son to do that shit?* he thought. *A Husband?*

Mary looked back in time to see the bearded Spanish driver shaking his head at her. She probably looked like a wet dog. *To hell with him!* She thought.

EXAMPLE OF THE THIRD-PERSON VIEW
IN THE PRESENT TENSE:

Mary is startled awake by the beeping of her cell phone. She reaches out and shuts it off. *God!* She thinks. *I can't believe morning's here already!*
She tosses aside the comforter and hears gusting wind; rain falls heavily. Mary Dean sits up; eases her legs over the side of her bed. Her left sock is missing.
The taint of something seeps into her bedroom. She must have fallen asleep after promising to put the trash in the garage.
She shuffles to the bathroom and looks at herself in the mirror. She doesn't like those lines at the side of her lips; doesn't like the darkness under her eyes. *Look like a raccoon. What's that spot on my neck? Was it there yesterday?*
"Mary Dean...you need to take care of yourself."
The garbage truck rumbles up the street. Mary hears it and swears. *The bin!* She hasn't put it on the sidewalk. She grabs a robe and dashes into the kitchen. She yanks the bag of trash out of its receptacle and runs for the garage.
As the door rumbles up, the morning chill stings her face. She runs to the side of the house where the large, wheeled bin is and tosses the kitchen trash in. She drags the bin, under the downpour, to the sidewalk just in time. The truck is just one house away.

Tony, the garbage truck driver, looks at her, drenched u8nder the downpour. He shakes his head but is glad she brought out her trash in time. *Hasn't* she *a son to do that shit?* he thinks. *A Husband?*

Mary looks back in time to see the bearded Spanish driver shaking his head at her. She probably looks like a wet dog. *To hell with him!* She thinks, self-consciously.

In closing, however, **points of view**, **tenses**, and knowing how to indicate **written thoughts** and **direct speech** are just tools in your writer's toolbox. Learn to use them and have fun putting together great fiction.

CONVO #5:

Fiction Writing is a Craft. There's No Doubt About It

Behind every great work of art is a craftsperson. So it is with the building of fiction. In this conversation, I'm going to compare writing to the craft of a house-builder—a carpenter. As such, I'll first look at ways to find a location to build a story. Following that will be a discussion on the importance of a work of fiction having a 'foundation'—the idea or premise that drives you to write your story. I will then talk about the significance of a narrative having a proper 'skeletal frame' or outline.

I will follow up by opening two specific toolboxes and together we'll examine the contents of each. The first contains sentence-writing implements (active and passive sentences along with the use of synonyms to curtail too-close repetition and clumsy flow); the second holds dialogue-writing tools.

By the end of this convo, you will be able to better set your story's location, achieve a stronger story-outline, juxtapose active and passive sentences effectively, make them read smoother, and manage your dialogue more effectively.

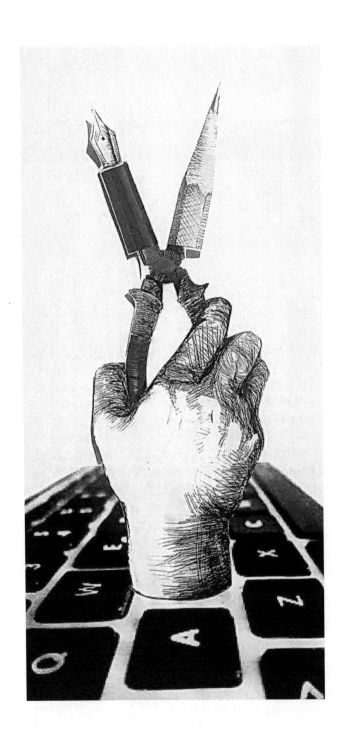

FICTION WRITING IS A CRAFT. THERE'S NO DOUBT ABOUT IT

A fiction writer is a storyteller. On a more hands-on level, however, a fiction writer is a craftsperson who uses words, phrases, and sentences to construct stories. The reason the word 'craft' can be applied to writing is that a writer builds narratives through plots in which characters react in situations calculated to keep a reader riveted to the end. The building of a story is very much like the building of a house. Let's examine this analogy:

One needs a location to build a house as one needs a location to set a story. *(Where will this story take place? In an office? In a hotel room? On an oil rig? On a deserted island?)*

LOCATION, LOCATION, LOCATION

For most writers, the easiest place to locate a story may well be a place they know best, like the city where they were born and grew. Of course, a writer might disguise their city—give it another name—add some fictional structures, and stuff like that. This is not uncommon. For many writers, it is an easy and natural choice. Stephen King, born in the state of Maine, set a lot of his novels in fictional locations there. William Faulkner set most of his novels in Lafayette County, Mississippi, even though he gave it a fictional name: Yoknapatawpha County, Mississippi. For many writers, 'location' forms the heart of their literary works.

Nothing, however, should stop you from setting your fiction in a location you have never visited, or in a location that doesn't exist. Think science fiction. As a young writer, I came across an essay by British novelist Desmond Bagley who instructed that with astute research, writers can set their fiction in places they have never ever visited in the flesh. One does not have to have visited the forests of Borneo, an island in Southeast Asia, to write a novel set in that location. The trick will be to immerse yourself in a series of National Geographic videos that show the flora and fauna of forests on that island and follow-up with general research on the people there in their social, cultural, and infrastructural settings—not excluding its politics and economics. After that, you will be able to combine the totality of your research with a great plot that takes place in a forest in Borneo. With your imagination tied to research, you can write a riveting novel in any location you choose.

LAYING THE FOUNDATION OF YOUR NOVEL

So, the location has been found, what comes next is the foundation onto which a house is constructed. Like that house, the plot for a novel also needs a foundation. But what is the foundation or premise of a work of fiction? In its simplest definition, the foundation or premise is that compelling idea that is interesting enough and has the potential to be developed into a riveting novel. Other teachers of creative writing, however, insist that the foundation or premise of a novel needs to be broken down into a single core-statement—a sentence that a writer must be able to articulate before starting on their plot. I do not subscribe to the 'single core-statement' approach, but will address it, regardless:

THE FOUNDATION OR PREMISE OF A NOVEL AS A SINGLE CORE-STATEMENT

My first novel, *"APATA: The story of a Reluctant Criminal"* is a manhunt story. But what was the core-statement that spawned it? Back then, had you asked me, I wouldn't have been able to articulate it. Back then, I didn't know what the hell a story's premise or foundation was. Ask me now, I'll say, **A man, despite how dark his skin is, can force you to see him as a man.** But even though I couldn't have articulated the above core-statement, it was etched somewhere deep within. And it came out passionately and morphed into a manuscript past 500 double-spaced typewritten pages long—from a laid-back prologue to a climax filled with echoes of gunshots and the finality of death, to an epilogue of bafflement.

I feel, very strongly, that the single-core-statement method can frustrate and cripple the creative impulse. Recently, I read that the single core-statement for the children's story, *"The Three Little Pigs"* written by James Halliwell-Phillipps is **"Foolishness leads to death and wisdom leads to happiness."** But did that author take the pains to write down the above before starting that story? I doubt it; this is my opinion because I am a writer like Halliwell-Phillipps was a writer. I don't know how many authors write like that. For me, it's too prescribed. Maybe there was just a passionate need in Mr. Halliwell-Phillipps to write a story that shows, through the plot's unfolding, that thoughtlessness can lead to death and insight to a satisfying end.

I am not telling you, however, that you should not try the single core-statement approach to write your plots; if it can work for you, why not? I'm just saying I have never used it and never will. For me, the stringency of it is too formulaic and mechanical. As such, I encourage most writers to explore the following **what if** method that is less rigid and a lot more fun to use:

HOW THE 'WHAT IF' METHOD WORKS TO FIND COMPELLING IDEAS FOR STARTING A NOVEL:

Many writers use this method to find the base idea to support entire novels. Let me demonstrate how it works. As I type these words, I glance at a picture of a skyscraper on the wall and I think, *"What if on its uppermost floor there's an office with a guy that most of his colleagues laugh at because he keeps a parachute under his desk?"* With that thought, do you believe I can create a whole novel based on it? Hell yes, I can—and so can you.

I can see a coworker—a very beautiful girl who has a jealous boyfriend who's a pilot but feels she's unfaithful to him and plans to fly his plane, 9-11 style, into his woman's building. In my mind, I can see all in the office, except the girlfriend and parachute-guy, perishing because he jumps with her. Maybe she's the only one who never laughed at him. See? My writer's mind has taken flight. I can create a whole plot based on the above **what if** question. It is a great way to find the foundation for a story.

One of the self-published novels I reviewed is entitled *"Final Notice"* by Van Fleisher. The plot centers around a medical device worn like a watch and tell a wearer when they're going to die. I can imagine that one day Van Fleisher thought, '*What if there was a medical watch that monitors a wearer's vital signs and tells them that they're going to die? ... What might they do?* (In the novel, all of the men who received their final notices chose to kill people they hated or people who wronged them.) This writer got a whole novel out of it. There's no question about it: the what if prompt works well. You can test it right now. Lay this book down and try a few *what if* questions of your own. It will be fun. It introduces a host of ideas that you will be able to exploit and come up with great plots for novels.

(Other than the *'what if'* method, a new writer is also encouraged to look at their own experiences in life and the life-experiences of others around them and use those experiences as *foundation*.)

Now, let's move on to the importance of having a strong plot outline for that novel you intend to write.

CREATING THE OUTLINE OR STRUCTURE OF YOUR NOVEL

With a house, its skeletal structure rises from the foundation. If that structure is weak it will collapse; so it is with a novel's plot-structure. Let's now look at a weak plot-outline and explore the needed thought-process to make it structurally strong. The one we're going to look at comes from an overseas-based writer who once contacted me for some assistance with her proposed novel. We agreed on a time when she would call. The following is a reconstruction of our telephone conversation:

"Give me an outline of it," I say to her.

"It's the story of a rich girl from Lagos, Nigeria," she begins, "the daughter of a wealthy and influential oil lawyer. She flees to America because she's being pursued by this notorious Nigerian drug dealer bent on raping her. After she lands in the USA, she learns that he and his gang have followed her."

"So, he follows her to the USA with the sole intent to rape her?"

"Yes," she says and continues: "So, in America, she hides in a suburb and hopes the Nigerian gangster doesn't find her. She lives incognito and falls in love with her neighbor, a handsome African American whom she hopes doesn't get killed because of her."

"Killed by the Nigerian drug dealer."

"Yes—because soon after finding a house in the suburb, she learns that he's found out where she lives."

"Can I ask you a few questions?"

"Of course."

"Before fleeing her country, does this rich Nigerian girl tell her wealthy father that she was being targeted by a local gangster?"

"I didn't factor that in. No."

"Let us say she did. Don't you think her father might have his armed, personal security protect his daughter? What do you think might have happened if she had told him?"

There's no response over the phone. I continue: "Of course, her father might have contacted the local police and the gangster might have been arrested or made to go on the run. But then, her dad may not have had to call in the police. His personal security team might have sought out the drug dealer and neutralized him. Then again, you say that she is rich too, so, she might have her own security to protect her. See where I'm going with this?"

There's no response from the other end. I press on: "With the points I just made, your entire plot-outline becomes pointless. This girl would have no reason to flee Nigeria. The gangster would not make it to America. And since this rich girl won't have to flee her country, she wouldn't be in an American suburb. As such, she won't meet the African American neighbor and fall in love with him. ... Are you there?"

"I see," the writer says.

I continue: "But let's take it that she indeed fled to the USA. Did she go into the Nigerian Embassy or Consulate and let them know that a Nigerian criminal, by name, had pursued her to the United States? Don't you think if she had, the Nigerian Authorities might have contacted US Immigration and made it known that a Nigerian criminal had entered the country with his gang and is bent on harming a Nigerian National on US soil? Don't you think the US Authorities would have nabbed them, jailed them all in the USA, and later deport them back to Lagos, in handcuffs?"

The writer sighs.

"What I'm hoping to show you," I say, gently, "is that your outline is not working. It doesn't hold up. ... To be honest, it doesn't make sense."

"But I showed that outline to a friend and she told me it was good," she insists.

"Your friend; is she a writer or a literary professional?"

"No, but she is a professor at the University."

"Is this a professor who teaches fiction writing?"

"Economics," she says.

"Fiction writing and economics are very different things, my friend."

She says nothing.

"Are you there?"

"Yes."

"So, what do you think of what I've told you?"

"Listen...thanks for your feedback, but I'm going to continue with my outline as it is—if you don't mind."

"Great speaking with you—best of luck, my dear."

I hang up.

Here was someone bent on writing the story *she* wanted to write even though from a real-world, real-life perspective her outline was absurd. But was she wrong to want to stick to her illogical plot? For thinking readers, she would be wrong.

But what if she was courting a readership steeped in the tradition of the most mediocre of films from Bollywood and Nollywood (Indian and Nigerian) movies that are blatantly illogical yet loved, regardless, by an adoring demographic?

At the end of the day, the choice you make overrides everything. To each their own. One, however, always gets out what one puts in.

Question: What would you do if after submitting your story's synopsis to a writing coach or a developmental editor, they tell you that your plot-outline doesn't make sense?

I'll tell you what you ought to do if you're serious about your writing: You rework that plot outline until it is firm, and then continue being vigilant for any glaring missteps on your writing journey.

Before you go, let me take you to my workspace and open a couple of toolboxes with some very handy literary wrenches that are old but still work well:

MY SENTENCE-WRITING TOOLBOX:

- Active sentences push your narrative along: *He grabbed and kissed her passionately.*

- Passive sentences do not push things: *Passionately, he grabbed and kissed her.*

- A paragraph of active sentences, however, can be as tedious to read as a paragraph of passive sentences. But a paragraph of active and passive sentences can be quite pleasing.

PARAGRAPH OF ALL-ACTIVE SENTENCES:

Alex gazes out the window. Sunlight streams through the double Venetian blinds. A lateral pattern of shadow and light falls on the faded burgundy carpet. Stillness waits on the flat top of the hedge outside the window. The cell phone by his elbow buzzes twice. He looks over and flips it open. He swears—sure it's yet another great-black-Friday-shopping reminder from Amazon. It is. He swears. Alex sighs and shakes his head.

PARAGRAPH OF ALL-PASSIVE SENTENCES:

Out of the window, Alex gazes. Through the double Venetian blinds, sunlight streams. On the faded burgundy carpet, a lateral pattern of shadow and light falls. On the flat top of the hedge outside the window, stillness waits. Twice, buzzes the cell phone by his elbow. After looking over at it, he flips it open. Thinking it's yet another black Friday shopping reminder from Amazon, he swears. Shaking his head, Alex sighs.

A PARAGRAPH OF ACTIVE AND PASSIVE SENTENCES:

Alex looks out the window. ***Through the double Venetian blinds, sunlight streams.*** A lateral pattern of shadow and light is on the faded burgundy carpet. ***On the flat top of the hedge outside, stillness waits.*** The cell phone by his elbow buzzes twice. He looks over and flips it open. ***Thinking it's yet another black Friday shopping reminder from Amazon, he swears.*** It is. Alex sighs and shakes his head.

Now, let us look at synonyms and how they can save us from sentences that flow clumsily—especially when we read them aloud. And what is it that causes clumsy flow? Nothing does it like too-close repetitions. Look at the following;

"The key reason one **novel** (1) receives a crappy review, and another **novel** (2) doesn't, always boils down to the quality of the story each **novel** (3) tells. If after a **novel** (4) is read, a *reviewer swears and wonders what the hell they're reading, your **novel** (5) stands to be rewarded with a one-star review."*

The word 'novel' appears five times in the above excerpt. Read it aloud and you'll hear how awkward it sounds. When we write today, we need to be aware that we may want to publish our titles as audiobooks. A text that reads smoothly is always best. The passage above as an audio excerpt would be tedious to listen to. So, how can we rewrite and fix it? The following can work:

To begin with, we:

1. Keep the first 'novel,'
2. We delete the second,
3. We replace the third with the word 'story,'
4. We replace the fourth with the word 'narrative,' and
5. Replace the final 'novel' with the word 'it.'

*"The key reason one **novel** receives a crappy review, and another doesn't, always boils down to the quality of the **story** each tells. If after a **narrative** is read, a reviewer swears and wonders what the hell they're reading, **it** stands to be rewarded with a one-star review."*

NOTE: There are times when a writer can eliminate a 'too-close repetition' problem by deleting one of the offending words and tighten the **sentence**. Let's look at the following: *"At the starting of a two-person dialogue sequence, it is important to establish the first **speaker** and second **speaker**."* By eliminating the first **'speaker'**, a tightened and better sentence will result: *"At the starting of a two-person dialogue sequence, it is important to establish the first and second **speaker**."*

MY DIALOGUE-WRITING TOOLBOX:

Is it okay to have two characters speaking minus a ton of dialogue tags? (*'He said, 'She said, 'He asked, etc., are dialogue tags*.) The answer is, yes, but it comes with a cautionary note:

If, for example, you want to do this with two speakers, you need to ensure that one speaker's speech is distinctly different from the other. Here's an example:

Nathaniel Wiley hated speaking up and this was because he stuttered badly. But today he had to say his piece. The fate of his farm was at stake and he had to stand tall and speak—despite the sniggers he knew he'd be forced to endure.

Hawthorne, the Chairman, who many believed acted as though he was a butler to the Royals, saw Wiley rising hesitantly.

"Please," Hawthorne said, waving his wooden hammer for order. "I see someone has an opinion."

Everyone looked at the ungainly Nathaniel Wiley turning his cap nervously in his hands.

"Come on now, Mr. Wiley—speak up, will you! You have the floor!"

"I b-b-beg to disagree, Sir!"

Someone suppressed a snigger.

"Disagree about what, my good fellow? What are you griping about?"

There was more chuckling.

"Y-Y-You d-damn well kno-know what I'm t-t-talking ab-ab-about, Haw-Hawthorne! The cho-cho-choice is m-m-mine t-t-to sell! A-a-and r-r-right now I f-f-feel we're b-b-being unfay-fairly p-p-preh-pressured to pah-part with w-w-what ours!"

"You say 'we'. But if so, my good man—why is it no one else shares your opinion? I'm curious."

"Tha-tha-that because th-they're f-f-fucking weak!"

"Oh My. Language, Mr. Wiley! Language! We do have women here, don't we?"

The above can go on and on with no dialogue handles necessary. It's a different matter, however, when two characters are speaking, and their speech styles are indistinct. This is when the writer needs to use dialogue handles and other devices to prevent readers from having to retrace spoken lines continually to ascertain who is speaking when. Here is an example of such a problem-prone scene:

> Sarah came over and sat tiredly over from Yvette.
> "You good, Sarah? **Yvette said.**
> "What do you think?" **Sarah said.**
> "It's going to be okay."
> "You think?"
> "Yes. I feel so. I don't think he's so callous."
> "There's so much about that guy you don't know. I want to tell you more, but I fear I'll start crying. Don't want that. I've been crying enough. People, I guess, are now sick of me!"
> "I'm not sure of that."
> "I'd be sick of me. Believe me."
> "People understand."
> "Oh, God! —I'm so hopeless...."

So, how do we fix the above? We can do so by adding more dialogue tags along with how things are expressed by using adverbs judiciously. We can add a bit on the physical appearance of one or both speakers as the conversation proceeds. We can help things by putting names within the lines. We can also allow the characters to interact physically as they speak. I've done all of the above in the following rewrite. Let's see how more effective it is:

> Sarah came over and sat tiredly over from Yvette.
> "You good, Sarah?" **Yvette said.**
> "What do you think?" **Sarah said, looking defeated.**
> "It's going to be okay."
> "You think?" **Sarah sighed again, despondently.**
> "Yes. I feel so. I don't think he's so callous."
> "**Yvette**, there's so much about that guy you don't know. I want to tell you more, but I fear I'll start crying. Don't want that. I've been crying enough. People, I guess, are now sick of me!"
> "I'm not sure of that," **Yvette said reassuringly.**
> "I'd be sick of me. Believe me."
> **Yvette reached out and touched Sarah's forearm gently.** "People understand."
> "Oh, God! —I'm so hopeless...." **Sarah said, her voice barely a whisper.**

NOW, LET US LOOK AT HOW SOME AUTHORS OVERWRITE AFTER SPECIFIC QUOTATION MARKS IN DIALOGUE:

*The old man, lips trembling, leveled his shotgun at Frank's chest. "Get out!" he **shouted**. "Get out of here before I shoot you!"*

In the above bit of dialogue, the exclamation mark denotes shouting. Writing he 'shouted' is therefore unnecessary once there is an exclamation mark. It might have been best to replace 'shouted' with **'snarled'**, **'snapped'**, or **'roared.'**

Let's look at the following:

*"How old are you, by the way?" she **asked**.*

In the above bit of dialogue, the word 'asked' is not necessary since a question mark denotes a question. It might have been best to replace the word 'asked' with 'said.'

But let us close those boxes for now and leave you with one reminder: Writing is a craft. Once you understand the tools and how to use them, you will begin to enjoy your literary crafting and make the best of it as a novice or a professional.

CONVO #6:

How an Acting Lesson Can Help Your Dialogue in Fiction

In this conversation, I begin with a theatrical exercise—one that compels a pair of performers to 'act' between their lines. Afterward, I will use the results of the exercise in a fictional excerpt to show how the dialogue you write can be enhanced with exposition.

HOW AN ACTING LESSON CAN HELP YOUR DIALOGUE IN FICTION

Let's observe HARRY, a stage director in a room, as he works with a pair of actors who never had formal training in stagecraft. We'll call them DAVID and SARAH.

They look on as Harry arranges two chairs and a little table as an improvised living room on the little stage. He demarcates where a door is for entry and exit. On a wall aback the arrangement, Harry draws a vertical rectangle and marks panes into it.

"Window," he mutters, turns, takes up a ruler, and continues. "Today, we're going to explore the idea that acting is what one actor does after hearing a line from another, even before responding with a line of their own. ...

"Any pair of individuals on a stage can trade lines woodenly from a given script. A true acting-student, however, will LISTEN to a line directed at them, THINK deeply about that line, and react with facial expressions or by way of body language before responding. The other actor does the same. So, we're going to explore the idea that good acting takes place between reciprocal lines of dialogue. Let's see what happens."

He turns to Sarah. "You have two lines: 'Molly died on the way here to see you,' and: 'I'm sorry.'"

He turns to David. "After she says her first line to you, I will start tapping time with this ruler. While doing so, you cannot speak. From the first tap, you start THINKING—internalizing what Sarah has told you. Let us see the LOOK on your face as you think of what you just heard. Let us see how what she told you affects your body-language—how it makes you move as what she tells you soaks into your consciousness as I tap. It is only when I stop tapping can you deliver your line—"

"Got it," David says. "What's my line?"

"Your line," Harry says, "is: 'Oh, my God! Oh, my God! Oh, my God! I can't believe it.' But listen carefully David ... if while you're saying your lines, I begin to tap once again, you must cease speaking and continue acting how you feel. Only when I stop tapping can you finish the line I interrupted. Understood?"

"So, your tapping," David says, "is primarily for me."
"Yes, just for you. Sarah will be reacting to whatever you do."
David nods. "We're ready."
"Lights!" Harry calls. Sarah approaches David.

SARAH: Molly ... died on the way here to see you....

HARRY BEGINS TAPPING.

Horror takes David's face.

THE TAPPING CONTINUES.

David sinks into a chair. He gazes at the floor.

THE TAPPING CONTINUES.

Tears settle in his eyes.

THE TAPPING CONTINUES.

Sarah comes over to him, rests a hand on his heaving shoulders.

THE TAPPING CONTINUES.

David covers his face and suppresses his sobbing.

THE TAPPING CONTINUES.

Sarah squeezes his shoulder.

THE TAPPING CONTINUES.

David erupts to his feet and moves to the window. There he continues to weep as Sarah stands back.

THE TAPPING STOPS.

DAVID: (Sobbing) Oh, my God! Oh, my God! Oh, My God! —

THE TAPPING RESTARTS.

David slumps in a corner and covers his face, sobbing.

THE TAPPING STOPS.

DAVID: Oh, my God!

Sarah consoles him.

SARAH: I'm sorry.

Beaming, Harry calls, "CUT! —Wow! That was amazing!"

I do believe writers can employ the above exercise to enhance their fictional dialogue. How so? This can be achieved by the writer getting into the head of every character, and once there, be, like David in the above exercise, and express, as David in his reactions to lines said. So, let's see how the above acting exercise with David and Sarah translates into fiction.

To begin with, I'll create a scene in which Sarah and David stand face-to-face and trade direct speeches devoid of pauses, breaks, or movement after her initial entry:

> Sarah enters the log cabin and stands before David.
> "Molly died on the way here to see you," she says.
> "Oh, my God! Oh, my God! Oh, My God!" says David. "Oh, my God!"
> "I'm sorry," says Sarah.

Four lines, thirty-eight words and not very emotional. Now, let us apply the results of the ruler-tapping exercise by typing all reactions to words heard in bold type:

Sarah enters the log cabin. **Her countenance tells David something is amiss. He furrows his brows.**

"Molly..." **The sides of Sarah's lips tremble.** "Molly died on the way here to see you...."

Horror takes David's face as he sinks into the chair behind him ... gazes emptily at the floor.

Sarah steps quickly over to him as tears settle in his eyes. She rests a hand gently on his shoulder.

David covers his face abruptly and begins sobbing, deeply and harshly.

Sarah squeezes his shoulder.

He erupts to his feet and moves to the window. There, he gazes into the snowy woods and weeps as Sarah stands back.

"Oh, my God! Oh, my God! Oh, My God!" **he groans in his grief as he turns and slumps down the rough cabin wall to the bearskin rug on the floor.** "Oh, my God!"

Sarah squats and hugs him. Now she is unable to hold back her tears. "I'm so sorry," she sobs.

Sixteen lines, fifty-six words and filled with emotion.

Good dialogue, when writing fiction, is more than mere spoken lines trapped between quotation marks traded woodenly between characters. The way individuals in a scene react to what other individuals say add dimension to exchanges.

CONVO #7:

How to Write Great Descriptive Scenes by Employing the 5 Human Senses

When writing descriptive scenes, some beginning writers tend to employ only two senses, the sense of SIGHT and the sense of HEARING. However, when writers add the senses of TOUCH (FEEL), SMELL, and TASTE, scenes leap off pages and become almost real for readers. The addition of touch, smell, and taste lend that special 'something' to a scene and blows readers away.

In this short conversation, I will create a scene in which only the senses of HEARING and SEEING are employed in the exposition. I'll then follow by rewriting the very scene with the sense of TOUCH (FEEL) added to it—followed with another rewrite with the sense of SMELL followed by a third rewrite with the sense of TASTE. As such, the culminating scene will carry all the human senses.

I hope it will be an exciting learning exercise for you.

HOW TO WRITE GREAT DESCRIPTIVE SCENES BY EMPLOYING THE 5 HUMAN SENSES

The following paragraph employs only what the protagonist, Emerson Chaney SEES and HEARS:

Emerson Chaney sat hunched in a cleft in the huge oak that towered above him and peered—unable to blink in his fear. **He saw something out there; he was sure—something huge and shaggy. A twig snapped just as he heard a booming thud like a monster's footfall.** He blinked. What the hell was that? Couldn't be a distant explosion. The old mine was too far away. **The booming sound came again.** Unconsciously, he was biting down on his lower lip. Whatever it was that approached was behind him now. He began to turn carefully with the double-barreled shotgun in his hands.

Now, let's add the protagonist's sense of TOUCH (FEEL) to it and see how better it makes the paragraph:

Emerson Chaney sat hunched in a cleft in the huge oak that towered above him and peered—unable to blink in his fear. He saw something out there; he was sure—something huge and shaggy. **The rough, cold texture of the tree's bark pressed into his bare right shoulder.** A twig snapped just as a dull, booming thud like a monster's footfall **vibrated through his body.** He blinked and **felt the sting of sweat in his eyes.** What the hell was that? Couldn't be a distant explosion. The old mine was too far away. The booming sound came again. Unconsciously, he was biting down on his lower lip. Whatever it was that approached was behind him now. With his **palms sweaty** on the long, double-barreled shotgun, he began to turn carefully.

Now, let us add his sense of SMELL to it:

Emerson Chaney sat hunched in a cleft in the huge oak that towered above him and peered—unable to blink in his fear. He saw something out there; he was sure—something huge and shaggy. The rough, cold texture of the tree's bark pressed into his bare right shoulder. **His unwashed sweatiness rising from below his collar assailed him.** A twig snapped just as a dull, booming thud like a monster's footfall vibrated through his body. He blinked and felt the sting of sweat in his eyes. What the hell was that? Couldn't be a distant explosion. The old mine was too far away. The booming sound came again. Unconsciously, he was biting down on his lower lip. Whatever it was that approached was behind him now. With his palms sweaty on the long, double-barreled shotgun, he began to turn carefully.

Now, let us add his sense of TASTE:

Emerson Chaney sat hunched in a cleft in the huge oak that towered above him and peered—unable to blink in his fear. He saw something out there; he was sure—something huge and shaggy. The rough, cold texture of the tree's bark pressed into his bare right shoulder. His unwashed sweatiness rising from below his collar assailed him. A twig snapped just as a dull, booming thud like a monster's footfall vibrated through his body. He blinked and felt the sting of sweat in his eyes. What the hell was that? Couldn't be a distant explosion. The old mine was too far away. The booming sound came again. Unconsciously, he was biting down on his lower lip. **It was when he tasted the salty blood that he knew it.** *He swore silently. Whatever it was that approached was behind him now. With his palms sweaty on the long, double-barreled shotgun, he began to turn carefully.*

When writers add the senses of TOUCH (FEEL), SMELL, and TASTE to their writing, scenes become almost real for readers. I hope the above samples prove this.

CONVO #8:

Would the Story of Your Life Make a Bestselling Book?

At some time or the other, I'm sure, you might have thought that you should tell the story of your life—convinced, deep in your being, that there would be no other story like it. And through the years many of us have written and continue to write autobiographies as self-published documentaries. One thing that drives many of us who self-publish our life-experiences, is a belief our stories would sell well and provide us passive income. How realistic is this?

In this conversation, we'll begin by examining the money-making chances of your autobiography. Next, I'll present a make-believe outline for a book based on the life of someone who has had a traumatic upbringing but who triumphed in the end. I'll then follow up by showing how the make-believe autobiographical outline, though commonplace, can be reworked to become the skeleton of a riveting story that stands to sell. Who knows, maybe at the end of this conversation you too can turn your life story into a mind-blowing novel.

WOULD THE STORY OF YOUR LIFE MAKE A BESTSELLING BOOK?

Many first-time writers start off by authoring books that document their successes after significant challenges in their lives. Time and again, I would get calls from individuals who think their life-experiences would make best-selling books—and every one of those calls go somewhat, like this:

"Mr. Bascom, I would like to discuss a literary project I have in mind that I'd like to run on you. Do you have time?"
"What's on your mind?
"I have a great idea for a book that you and I could do together."
"What will it be about? —Tell me more."
"My life-story. I'm sure if it's written it will be a best-seller..."

So, let's talk about this. Will that personal story you feel you must write make a bestseller? Chances are it *may* sell. It becoming a 'bestseller' is another matter. Frankly, it depends on who you are. With autobiographies, this is how it goes in two questions:

ARE YOU A HOT CELEBRITY STILL MAKING HEADLINES?
Yes? Chances are, your book will sell.

ARE YOU A WASHED-OUT CELEBRITY MOST HAVE FORGOTTEN?
Yes? Your book may not sell very well.

Fame and notoriety sell books; spicy 'tell-alls' on celebrities can be hot sellers. No doubt about it, the lifestyles of the rich and famous are lucrative literary properties. The run-of-the-mill despair-and-survival stories of ordinary folk do not. The world, apparently, is not interested in the life experiences of ordinary people; it has grown indifferent to stories of individuals who were abused, addicted, molested but made it, nonetheless. If you're just a regular Joe Blow or Jane Pain and wrote an autobiography of the horrible life you've had from a child but overcame it all and became successful, most may read the tear-jerker of a blurb and think, 'Who the hell cares? I have enough dramas of my own to think about.'

Let's look at a make-believe outline of an autobiography someone who's not a celebrity might put out:

My name is Vincent. My story starts before my birth. My mother is a sexually abused teenager who has grown to become a prostitute and drug addict. From time to time she would have volatile relationships with mostly ex-cons and criminals. She's also having countless run-ins with the law because of her drug use. She is beautiful but is never allowed to show it: Her face is always swollen from knuckle-blows and back-handed slaps.

After countless abortions, she gets pregnant once again and for some Godly reason decides to keep the child that is destined to be me. One night a 'John' is thrashing her mercilessly with the buckled end of a thick leather belt. She thinks she's going to die. She pulls a long-bladed kitchen knife from under a mattress and plunges it into her client's throat. He dies gurgling blood on a carpeted motel floor. She's arrested, taken to jail, ends in prison. It's where I am born. My mom dies soon after and I end in the foster system.

I turn out to be a quiet and brilliant boy child whom one of the social workers becomes fond of. She adopts me legally and she becomes my mother. I grow, by and by, into a seemingly ambitious young man.

Soon, I fall in love with sixteen-year-old Britney who, unknown to me, strips at a local club after school. One night she introduces me to weed. I want to please her, so I take a few pulls and it gets me very sick. My mother smells marijuana in my clothes after I get home. She sits me down and reveals something to me for the first time: She tells me my origins—tells me that Britney's path is destined to be my birth mother's path; tells me not to be part of such a cycle. The talk opens my eyes.

I begin to see multiple versions of Britney—girls like her, all around—Britneys getting pregnant, Britneys turning tricks, Britneys being with meth dealers ... Britneys going nowhere. I know from my gut that I do not want to be part of the vicious cycle that many here accepted as life.

Britney realizes that I'm done with her and tries to get me to be with her once again; nothing works. She feels scorned and rejected—feels I think I'm better than her and gets her brother and his friends to teach me a lesson. They surround me with knives and with chains wrapped around their fists. An old friend from the orphanage pulls up, draws a gun and dares them to touch me. They leave. The next day my rescuer is found battered to death in the playground.

I tell my mom I couldn't live where we were any longer, and she leaves with me. We start living somewhere else where there are trees and open, grassy spaces. I start going to college; I graduate, find a great job, fall in love with a wonderful girl, and we live happily ever after.

The autobiographical outline above—something I quickly put together—can be replicated, in truth, by many who have had such traumatic journeys and have survived. Such stories, unfortunately, have become much too common—so common they are regarded with indifference. But is the above outline worthless for a book? No, it is not. Nothing should stop you from writing and publishing your challenges and your successes. It will be a lasting record, a mark that you lived and overcame. Might it sell well? Beyond the circle of your family, relatives, and supportive friends, it may not.

But as I said in my brief intro, there *are* ways for someone to take their autobiographical outline and use it as the base of another story that stands to make some money. Let's take Vincent's outline above and see how that can happen. We can:

1: **Change the protagonist:**

The protagonist does not have to be a human person. What if 'Vincent' is an alien?

(My name is Dionamuh, I am a naamoh from the planet Heerah in a recently discovered galaxy beyond your Milky Way. My story starts before my hatching. My mother is an egg-burdened female of my species. She has grown to become an Etuit (what is called a prostitute on earth) and tiddagurd (a drug addict).
...

Or, what if 'Vincent' is an animal? An animal? Why not? Let's do the research. I just did the following keyword search: *Sexual abuse and rape in the animal kingdom*. One of the results is an article entitled, *'7 Adorable Animals that are Also Murderous Monsters.'* It tells that dolphins and ducks are among a group of animals not as 'cute' as they seem—that they are extremely sexually aggressive. So, why not take the Vincent story, rework it, and make it the outline for a dramatic dolphin tale? The following is my take. I call it...

VINDOLPH'S WORLD © Harold A. Bascom, 2018

My name is Vincent. I am a bottle-nosed boy dolphin. My story starts before my birth as a calf in a marine park. My mother is a sexually abused girl dolphin who has grown to become a smooth, beautiful dolphin cow most of the other bull dolphins in our pod, are attracted to. They bully and force her to mate with them. It starts after a mean bull named Big Snout who, with his two friends, Rama and Shrillock, separate my mom from some other female dolphins and force her to have sex with them. They threaten her and rake her skin with their teeth until she cannot stop them. They take turns raping her and abusing her. Whenever she tries to escape, they would catch her and bloody her some more. The other females would not help my mom. She's beautiful but is never allowed to show it. Her skin is always scarred and black and blue from being hit by the snouts of bulls in heat.

After two of my mom's calves are killed by Big Snout and his friends, she continues to be raped again and again. Then she gets pregnant with another calf. One night, Shrillock, one of Big Snout's mean friends, circles my mom with a greedy look in his eyes. She knows his next move would be to beat her about until I am dead in her tummy; then he'll be mating with her. She decides to protect me. She swims off, turns and attacks suddenly like a torpedo. She drills her bony snout into his head with all her might, rapturing his brain and killing him.

She's taken away and placed in an isolated cage where she falls seriously ill. The humans deliver me and call me a miracle. My mom dies immediately after. The humans keep me separated until I am a strong bull—huge as Big Snout. Maybe I'm his son. Then they put me back with the rest of the herd.

I turn out to be a quiet and brilliant young dolphin. I grow close to the girl-trainer who took me from my mother's tummy. One day she speaks to me and we understand each other. Because I can communicate with the human, I become very popular— more popular than Big Snout who wants to know how I was able to speak to the girl human. So, he tells his daughter, Britney, to be friends with me—and I'm happy. Britney is the most beautiful girl dolphin in the herd.

Soon I fall in love with her. But Britney, unknown to me and her dad, flirts with most of the boy dolphins who starts feeding her a strange weed in the water that makes a girl dolphin horny. There are times I feel so jealous I'm always thinking of fighting some other bull dolphin. Then one day, I challenge a big young bull who was all over Britney. Big Snout, swims up, asks me why I would think to fight his son. I tell him his son is mating with Britney. Big Snout gets angry and tells me his daughter is pure and nothing like my mom was. I get angrier and tell him his daughter is a wild, willing whore. He darts at me, but he's not as strong and fast as he once was. I'm too quick for him. He misses me with his snout. I pivot as he swims by, hit him with my strong young tail then jab him out of the water. He squeals in pain as his friends, led by Rama starts for me. The girl-scientist sees and tells me to swim for my life. She opens a cage and I bolt for it. Once inside she locks me to safety.

My human friend sits at the side of my cage and tells me what I do not know about my mom about her life, about how she was abused by Big Snout and his friends, and how hard it was for her to make me, and how she died after they took me out of her battered body. Then she tells me she knows I love Britney, but that Britney is not good for me, that if I mated with her, I may lose my ability to communicate with humans. She opens my eyes.

I begin to see multiple versions of young female dolphins like Britney all over the large aquarium—Britneys getting pregnant, Britneys turning tricks, Britneys with mean young bulls only wanting to fight and mate ... Britneys going nowhere. I know from my gut that I do not want to be part of the vicious cycle that many accept as life in the aquarium. I tell my human friend that I'm ready to come back to the herd—that I'm not afraid. She lets me out.

Britney tries to get me to notice her, but it doesn't work. She feels rejected and asks me who the hell I think I am—if I think that being able to speak to the human makes me better than the rest of them. Britney gets Rama and her brothers to teach me a lesson. They surround me with the intent to mob me—batter me. Just then, Big Snout, still wounded, surfaces and dares them to hurt me. They turn away murmuring to one another. The next day Big Snout is found battered and broken and dead.

My human friend lets me into a cage. She tells me it's not safe for me to be in the open Aquarium any longer. Soon after, she takes me to live in a warm, open ocean where there is no garbage and the water is not oily. And there, I live happily ever after.

 # 2: Change the location or time period of your outline:

I could have easily taken the made-up plot-outline of 'Vincent's and made it something happening on another planet. I could have made it a prehistoric story or a futuristic story.

IN CONCLUSION

The possibilities of taking your autobiographical outline and turning it into something else are limitless. The lesson for you here is that, whatever your life story may be, you can choose to use it as the foundation plot for something else—something unique that might gain more literary mileage—gain general readership. Countless readers are fascinated by the unique, especially if that unique 'something' is grounded in an identifiable reality. And always remember, where there is creativity, there is hope.

But let me close by repeating: IF YOU FEEL VERY STRONGLY THAT THE STORY OF YOUR LIFE AS IT IS WILL MAKE YOU A BESTSELLER—THEN WRITE IT. Just make sure you follow the guidelines offered in other chapters in this book and make your manuscript shine.

CONVO #9:

How to find the ART in Rewriting

I always thought the Hemingway quote, 'The only kind of writing is rewriting' or the more generic form of it, 'The art of writing is rewriting,' was gospel to all who wrote fiction. But then I came upon a young writer who boasted that he was so good with words, he had no need to rewrite anything. I met him a few years ago and have since been searching for the publication of his magnum opus, for surely his literary genius, by and by, was destined to be recognized and celebrated worldwide. I never found a single published book of his; maybe I missed it.

I am not a 'talented' or 'genius' writer. I struggle to string a group of sentences together. I'm never satisfied at the first go. I would rewrite again and again as I vacillate between the active and passive forms and would do this until the flow of a paragraph sounds right.

In this conversation I'm going to try something different: In the course of my talk, I'll be doing rewrites of my sentences as we go along. It will be, hopefully, as if you're looking over my shoulders as I write and rewrite.

I'll also be speaking about how many rewrites of a manuscript it takes to arrive at a final draft. I'll also speak on specific things you need to focus on when doing novel-manuscript rewrites. Then I'll end by cataloging a series of quotations by famous writers on the importance of rewriting.

FINDING THE 'ART' IN REWRITING

What exactly is rewriting? It is precisely as it denotes: the rewriting of sentences, paragraphs, dialogue, and chapters, etc. We choose to rewrite because we need to make our sentences better. We rewrite them because we know that expressive sentences make improved paragraphs and that stringing-together rich paragraphs result in great chapters. For passionate writers who crave perfection, rewriting drives us.

That last sentence feels too passive. I'll rewrite it:

Rewriting drives passionate writers who crave perfection.

I'm still not satisfied. Let me try again:

Passionate writers who crave perfection, rewrite intensely.

Still not satisfied:

Passionate writers, driven by a need for perfection, rewrite intensely.

I'm happy.

HOW MANY DRAFTS DOES IT TAKE TO END AT A FINAL MANUSCRIPT?

It's different for every writer. It took me three drafts to complete the manuscript of *APATA: The Story of a Reluctant Criminal* submitted to Heinemann Educational Books of London. **MANUSCRIPT DRAFT #1** was less than three hundred, double-spaced typewritten pages—a product of month after month of grueling writing. This was because it was my first attempt at writing a novel. I had only written short stories before. In the end, it was a rough, uncertain batch of type-written pages, but I knew it. Draft #1 was the one that a few friends, who were also vying to be writers, read and offered their critiques.

I started rewriting to make it better because I knew I could. It became **MANUSCRIPT DRAFT #2** that I improved on, continually adding new characters and situations in it—pushing the boundaries of the story to ensure that I made at least 300 double-spaced typewritten pages before writing 'The End.' At that point, manuscript-draft #2 was over 400 typewritten pages.

By the time Heinemann replied to my query letter and said they had no objections to looking at a manuscript submitted from South America, I was into **MANUSCRIPT DRAFT #3**. It had reached 500-plus typewritten pages. It became **SUBMISSION MANUSCRIPT #1**.

Once it was accepted, I began working along with a Heinemann developmental editor and later a Heinemann copy editor until the submission manuscript became page proofs that were proofread. The printed book followed, and I became a published author.

Rewriting is a show of no-compromise; the process is priceless.

IF YOU SAY TO ME, "WHAT EXACTLY DO YOU FOCUS ON WHEN YOU'RE REWRITING?" I'LL ANSWER WITH THREE WORDS: "SENTENCES, WORDS, PHRASES."

I look at my paragraphs for active-passive rhythm. When I write I make sure that there are both active and passive sentences in my paragraphs. I love to play them against the other. I am also a writer who believes that when my sentences are read there should be a cadence to them—something I picked up from the style of John Steinbeck and love of poetic prose.

I might also isolate a specific word in a sentence and wonder if it is appropriate and communicates exactly what I mean to say.

Let us consider the following sentence taken from CONVO #5, and take note of the emboldened word:

But what if she was courting a readership steeped in the tradition of the most mediocre of films from Bollywood and Nollywood (Indian and Nigerian) movies that are **wantonly** *illogical yet loved, regardless, by an adoring demographic?*

Something bothered me about the word 'wantonly.' Something about it felt off. I quickly looked up its synonyms. It also meant 'lustfully,' 'promiscuously,' and 'lasciviously.' The latter words were too far from what I needed to express. So I rewrote it and was happy:

But what if she was courting a readership steeped in the tradition of the most mediocre of films from Bollywood and Nollywood (Indian and Nigerian) movies that are **blatantly** *illogical yet loved, regardless, by an adoring demographic?*

If I suspect a specific sentence might confuse a reader, I would rewrite for clarity. I would try my very best to say something as simple as I can. When rewriting for clarity and simplicity, I always think of a legendary story from Guyana, South America, *"The Verbose Prophet and the Schoolboy"*, and it always keeps me honest when I'm rewriting sentences for simplicity and clarity. Let me take a break here to tell the above story:

But first, I think I need to rewrite the above paragraph:

I also look at my sentences for redundancies—things that may cause a reader to wonder what the hell I'm trying to say. I would rewrite for clarity. I would try my best to say something as simple as I can. When rewriting for clarity and simplicity, I always think of a story that comes from a rural area of Guyana, South America. It is one that always keeps me honest when I'm rewriting sentences for simplicity and clarity. Let me tell it:

THE VERBOSE PROPHET AND THE SCHOOLBOY

Once upon a time, there was a gentle lunatic who lived in a coastal village in the country of Guyana, South America. Everyone called him 'Prophet Wills.' People in the village said that he had studied too much and because of it became insane.

One day, the principal of a village-school became ill and couldn't be there to supervise classes. Someone suggested that Prophet Wills took charge of the school for the day, and the Village Council agreed.

After he arrived at the school, Prophet Wills stood on a deck overlooking the yard where the children milled. He held a large brass bell in his hand. He looked down to the children and pointed to a boy in a red shirt.

"JUVENILE!" he called.

A teacher touched the boy. "Mr. Wills is calling you," she said.

"My name is not Juvenile," the boy said.

The teacher laughed. "Juvenile just means 'youngster.' He's calling you."

The boy skipped up the stair to Prophet Wills who held out the bell to him. The boy took it, and Prophet Wills said to him, "Tintinnabulate the metallic instrument—and let it procure melodious sounds!"

The boy, open-mouthed, stammered, "Wha-what, Sir?"

The teacher shouted to the boy, "Ring the bell!"

The boy rang the bell.

The pupils below formed orderly lines and prepared to proceed to their respective classes.

With the above story ever in mind, I would try my very best to say something as simple as I can. I always try to write *Ring the bell* instead of *Tintinnabulate the metallic instrument—and let it procure melodious sounds*. I always push beginning authors to rewrite for simplicity. On many occasions I have come across prose, so convoluted, I've had to say to a new writer, "In simple words, what are you trying to say?" And every time that new writer would reply with a sentence as simple as, 'Ring the bell.' I would say to them, "Then write that." That's when I would tell the above story. And after the laughter wanes, I would exhort them to read Hemingway.

I END WITH A SERIES OF QUOTATIONS BY FAMOUS WRITERS ON THE PROCESS OF REWRITING. ENJOY AND BE INSPIRED:

KURT VONNEGUT
Your eloquence should be the servant of the ideas in your head. Your rule might be this: If a sentence, no matter how excellent, does not illuminate your subject in some new and useful way, scratch it out.

STEPHEN KING:
When your story is ready for rewrite, cut it to the bone. Get rid of every ounce of excess fat. This is going to hurt; revising a story down to the bare essentials is always a little like murdering children, but it must be done.

HELEN DUNMORE:
Reread, rewrite, reread, rewrite. If it still doesn't work, throw it away.

LARRY L. KING:
Write. Rewrite. When not writing or rewriting, read. I know of no shortcuts.

CATHRYN LOUIS:
Rewriting is the crucible where books are born.

MICHAEL CRICHTON:
Books aren't written – they're rewritten. Including your own. It is one of the hardest things to accept, especially after the seventh rewrite hasn't quite done it.

FRANCINE PROSE:
Among the questions that writers need to ask themselves in the process of revision–Is this the best word I can find? Is my meaning clear? Can a word or phrase be cut from this without sacrificing anything essential? —perhaps the most important question is: Is this grammatical?

JOHN IRVING:
More than a half, maybe as much as two-thirds of my life as a writer is rewriting. I wouldn't say I have a talent that's special. It strikes me that I have an unusual kind of stamina.

TED SOLOTAROFF:
Writing a first draft is like groping one's way into a dark room, or overhearing a faint conversation, or telling a joke whose punchline you've forgotten. As someone said, one writes mainly to rewrite, for rewriting and revising are how one's mind comes to inhabit the material fully.

JOHN UPDIKE:
Writing and rewriting are a constant search for what it is one is saying.

SAUL BELLOW:
The main reason for rewriting is not to achieve a smooth surface, but to discover the inner truth of your characters.

ERNEST HEMINGWAY:
I rewrote the ending of 'Farewell to Arms' 39 times before I was satisfied.

JOHN CASEY:
Writing is rewriting; rewriting is writing—from the first crossed-out word in the first sentence to the last word inserted above a caret, that most helpful handwritten stroke.

BERNARD MALAMUD:
I would write a book or a short story, at least three times–once to understand it, the second time to improve the prose, and a third to compel it to say what it still must say.

SIDONIE GABRIELLE COLETTE:
Sit down and put down everything that comes into your head and then you're a writer. But an author is one who can judge his own stuff's worth, without pity, and destroy most of it.

RICHARD NORTH PATTERSON:
Writing is rewriting. A writer must learn to deepen characters, trim writing, intensify scenes. To fall in love with the first draft to the point where one cannot change it is to greatly enhance the prospects of never publishing.

CONVO #10

Cliché Hunting: How to Identify Them in Your Writing and Fix Them with Extreme Prejudice

In this conversation, we're going to look at clichés, which are phrases that are 'overused and betray a lack of original thought.' Beginning writers of fiction hoping to be recognized as capable, need to avoid clichés **like the plague**. *In the latter sentence, the phrase 'like the plague' is a cliché. I will replace it with something original. Here goes: Beginning writers of fiction hoping to be recognized as capable, need to avoid clichés* **like a YouTube thumbs-down.**

Since the use of clichés in fiction writing is frowned upon in all literary circles, the goal of this conversation will be about the need to isolate and replace them in your writing. I will begin, however, by speaking a little on how clichés can be identified. Afterward, I will then use each of the five clichés listed below in an excerpt and then rewrite each excerpt with the cliché replaced by an original phrase.

#1: **The news spread like wildfire.**
#2: **Action speaks louder than words.**
#3: **Behind every dark cloud is a silver lining.**
#4: **Like two peas in a pod.**
#5: **In the nick of time.**

After the above exercise, you'll be guided to where on the Internet you'll find a comprehensive list of clichés in alphabetical order.

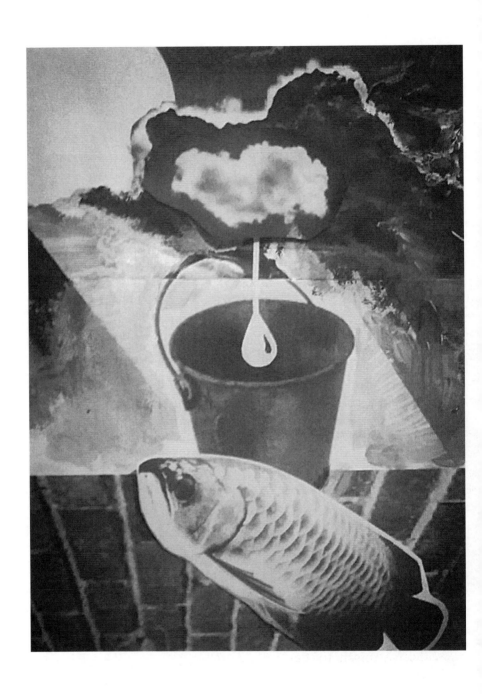

CLICHÉ HUNTING: HOW TO IDENTIFY THEM IN YOUR WRITING AND FIX THEM WITH EXTREME PREJUDICE

In this convo, clichés and their replacements are in bold, italic type. One excerpt with a cliché will be followed by the same excerpt with the cliché replaced. So, let's begin:

An error must first be recognized before it can be fixed; so how does a new writer identify a cliché in their manuscript? The answer may lie in a writer's ear. How many times have you sat in a meeting and heard a speaker introduced as having **"taken some time from their busy schedule to be here..."** or seen a speaker tap a microphone nervously and say, **"Is this thing on?"** or heard that speaker make a promise to **"leave no stone unturned..."** to achieve some promise made? Every one of the latter phrases in bold italics is a tired cliché.

Unfortunately, clichés find themselves in our writing and that's not always good. Fact is, clichés are all around us. We *think* them and use them; our neighbors *think* them and use them; our coworkers *think* them and use them: Clichés are pervasive:

Brad glances over to the cubicle over from his and sees the obvious: Grace and Andrew together—shoulder to shoulder. He shakes his head and thinks they're indeed **like two peas in a pod.** CLICHÉ ALERT!

Melanie spots Errol having a conversation with Phil at the coffee machine. Errol! ... She recalls that in their last group-project he was useless—did not contribute a single idea to the pool. She saw him as **the fifth wheel to a coach.** CLICHÉ ALERT!

Now, let's get to the five clichés listed in the introduction—let's see how we might fix each after they appear in the following passages:

CLICHÉ #1: *THE NEWS SPREAD LIKE WILDFIRE.*

The news of the terrorist attack on the twin towers ***spread like wildfire*** in Jersey City. Soon, it seemed everyone came out to look toward the New York City skyline with apprehensive faces.

Let us rewrite and replace the above cliché:

Every TV station broke their programming to show the planes striking the twin towers. Soon, it seemed everyone in Jersey City came out to look toward the New York City skyline with apprehensive faces.

How would *you* fix cliché #1?

CLICHÉ #2: *ACTION SPEAKS LOUDER THAN WORDS.*

All except the old actor at the back were yakking—telling the new director how each felt the scene might work best. The grey-haired veteran, with the smallest part in the play, just leaned back in his chair and listened until he thought he had heard enough noise. He slowly raised a hand and waved.

"Hold it everyone!" snapped Adolph Fisher the stage director, "Mr. Williams wants to say something!"

A hush fell on the rehearsal space. Everyone looked at the veteran actor as he rose to his feet.

"You've all been giving the director suggestions," he said, "but if each of you has an idea—why not pair with someone and show the fucking director what you feel would work. Jesus!"

There were murmurs and nods, all around.

*The director was grateful that Mr. Williams spoke up; he, Fisher, always believed that **action spoke louder than words**.*

Let's try the following fix:

> The director was grateful that Mr. Williams spoke up; he, Fisher always believed that **too much talk without action was an aching waste of time.**

I can also try this:

> The director was grateful that Mr. Williams spoke up; he, Fisher, always believed that **demonstrating something made more sense.**

Or maybe this:

> The director was grateful that Mr. Williams spoke up. Fisher always believed **that shutting the fuck up and showing some shit was more productive.**

How would *you* fix cliché #2?

CLICHÉ #3: *BEHIND EVERY DARK CLOUD IS A SILVER LINING.*

> One week after her unemployment ran out, Clarisse Horton did an interview and landed herself a job at the bowling alley. After she received the good-news call from the manager, she dropped to her knees and wept. It had been so long she had been praying for something good to happen for her. She had come close to thinking that her prayers constituted part of an empty, silly ritual and that her brother, Cob, was probably right: that there was no invisible bearded white dude that looked out for poor white trash like themselves. But now her faith in God had been renewed and her conviction in the fact that **behind every dark cloud is a silver lining** was now unshakable.

Let's try the following fix:

...But now her faith in God had been renewed and her conviction in the fact that **good things come to those who wait** was now unshakable.

But wait a minute, Harold (I'm talking to myself—which I do a lot. Lol), you replaced a cliché with a cliché: *Good things come to those who wait.* Damn! I need to rewrite:

*…But now her faith in God had been renewed and her conviction in the fact that **trying times do not last forever** was now unshakable.*

How would *you* fix cliché #3?

CLICHÉ #4: *LIKE TWO PEAS IN A POD.*

*Brad glances over to the cubicle over from his and sees the obvious: Grace and Andrew together—shoulder to shoulder. He shakes his head and thinks they're indeed **like two peas in a pod**.*

Let's try the following fix:

*Brad glances over to the cubicle over from his and sees the obvious: Grace and Andrew together—shoulder to shoulder. He shakes his head and thinks they're indeed **like interlaced fingers**.*

CLICHÉ #5: *IN THE NICK OF TIME.*

Through the flames of the burning car, the two policemen spotted the unconscious figure of the woman behind the wheel.
"Oh, God! It's going to blow!" screamed someone.
*The lawmen, however, were not deterred, they reached into the licking flames and smoke, grabbed the woman, and pulled her from the burning vehicle **in the nick of time**.*
The gas tank exploded.

Let's try the following fix:

*The lawmen, however, were not deterred, they reached into the licking flames and smoke, grabbed the woman, and pulled her from the burning vehicle **with a few minutes to spare**.*

The gas tank exploded.

BUT ARE THERE *ANY* INSTANCES WHEN IT'S OKAY FOR A WRITER TO USE CLICHÉS?

The answer is yes. Let's look at the following excerpt:

> *All except the old actor at the back were yakking—telling the new director how each felt the scene might work best. The veteran, with the smallest part in the play, just leaned back in his chair and listened until he thought he had heard enough noise. He slowly raised a hand and waved the palm.*
> *"Hold it everyone!" snapped Adolph Fisher the stage director, "Mr. Williams wants to say something.*
> *A hush fell on the rehearsal space. Everyone looked at the veteran actor as he rose to his feet.*
> *"You've all been giving the director suggestions," he said, "but if each of you has an idea—why not pair with someone and show the fucking director what you feel would work.* **Action speaks louder than words***. Isn't that shit still true? Jesus!"*
> *There were murmurs and nods, all around.*
> *The director was grateful that Mr. Williams spoke up. Fisher always believed that shutting the fuck up and showing some shit was more productive.*

In the above case in which a cliché is used within dialogue, it is quite okay. People speak in different ways and some use clichés. It may even be part of a specific speech characteristic of someone in your manuscript, so, why not? As a writer, however, you need to make yourself more and more aware of clichés and be extremely vigilant. They have a way of popping up in your exposition. This is because there are so many of them, you couldn't possibly know them all. The keywords below will lead you to an online article by Ms. Lisa Lepki, entitled *'List of Clichés.'* It is comprehensive, in alphabetical order, and will assist you in finding and fixing them in your work. To find this list, simply type the following keywords into your browser: **'what is a cliché and why should you avoid them**.*'* Have fun.

CONVO #11

Where Do Ideas for the Plots of Short Stories and Novels Come From?

*Every guest author to literary forums comes prepared to answer the question, "Where do you get your ideas from?" In this conversation, I'll speak on how ideas for my fictional work are generated and I'll do so in a unique way. I will allow you to read two of my not-yet-published short stories. Their names are, "**The Thermostat**", and, "**Lousy Cat**." After each, I reveal whatever it was (or whatever there were) that spawned the story. By the end of this convo, I hope you will find new inspirational sources for your fiction.*

The Thermostat

By Harold A. Bascom

In the height of the summer, Rhonda Brown dressed in layers, but only in her department where the thermostat was always set by her supervisor, Kevin Carter, who liked it cool: sixty degrees. Rhonda's coworkers laughed at her continual complaints that the office was kept too damn cold. Most in the office didn't seem to mind the chilliness that turned the tips of Rhonda's dark fingers to prunes. When she began walking with a small heater to work, they laughed even harder and thought she was a piece of work.

The only other person-of-color in the office was Chanise Griffin, a girthy African American woman who sat closest to Rhonda. Chanise laughed with Kevin when they were in each other's faces, but when he was out of sight, she'd repeatedly mutter to Rhonda that she couldn't wait to see his white ass fired.

Chanise hated Kevin; the feelings between them were mutual: They had 'history'—a bad one. She even had him written up for assault: she accused him of shoving her. He countered by writing her up for cursing him to his face in front of staff. Both were properly reprimanded and warned of termination. And so, for their jobs' sake, they feigned getting along.

Rhonda had just settled in the relatively cozy break room with a diet soda and a tuna sandwich from the cafeteria when Chanise, with a heaped tray of junk, joined her.

"I guess you're truly suffering in there, huh?" Chanise said with a toss of her obese head to indicate their office around a corner from the corridor.

Rhonda shrugged. "The day will soon be over."

"I would have lodged a complaint to Human Resources!" Chanise said, raising a heavily stacked hamburger to her face.

"To what end? They're not going to touch that thermostat for me, Chanise. Trust me. Don't you notice how Mulroney's always saying that the temperature in the room needs to be low for the sake of the computer equipment?

"I don't know why Pat would spout that crap! She just sides with Kevin on everything—always up in his face!" Then below her breath: "And a married woman at that!"

"Not going there, Chanise." Rhonda hated workplace gossip.

"The head guy in Transportation is your people, a Caribbean guy, and he says the thermostat in his department is never low as in our office. Don't they have computerized equipment too?"

"Maybe I'll talk to Kevin about bringing the temperature level up."

"Best of luck with that," Chanise murmured through a mouthful of cheesecake.

"He has done it a few times for me before, but soon after, someone would lower it again."

"No one else but that Pat!"

"I don't know, Chanise." Rhonda looked at her coworker. "Would you believe leaving this job keeps crossing my mind?"

"No!"

"Yep. Talked to my husband about it, last night."

"And what Gordon said?"

"He laughed. Said someone leaving a job because of a thermostat is downright ridiculous."

"He's not wrong, Rhonda! You need to fight them!"

Rhonda laughed. She looked at the large digital clock on the wall with the painting of a dilapidated Southern Mansion and got to her feet. "Time," she muttered.

How do I fight them? Rhonda thought, back at her desk. It wasn't that Chanise was getting to her; the cold was. Her portable heater had stopped working earlier. Now, she couldn't feel below her knees. And with her diabetes too, she thought she needed to be less passive. The temperature on the thermostat needed to be pushed up; she would have asked Kevin to do so, but he had been called to the office of their department's director, Fred Carmichael. (Chanise had whispered to Rhonda that Fred looked pissed when he appeared in the doorway to the office floor and beckoned to Kevin. Chanise had murmured gleefully, "I hope he's about to get his inept ass chewed-out in Fred's office for some new nonsense he did!")

Rhonda got to her feet, walked past Chanise, food-messy at her desk, avoided Pat Mulroney, the Southern woman with the prominent ass, past Charles whom most thought was bipolar, and reached up to the thermostat off to the left of Kevin's desk.

"WHAT THE HELL YOU THINK YOU'RE DOING?"

Rhonda Brown turned to a red-faced, Kevin Carter. He had never spoken to her like that before.

A sudden hush fell into the office. The low hum of the air-conditioning system came through with the sound of a child laughing as though being tickled in the nearby cafeteria.

Rhonda composed herself. "Are you speaking to me, Kevin? —you couldn't be speaking to me!"

"I-I'm sorry," Kevin was saying.

But Rhonda only heard the voice of her husband from the night before:

"What the hell's wrong with you, eh? ...

"Why are you always afraid to stand up for your own rights, Rhonda? ...

"You think if the temperature was affecting anyone else in that office the way it's affecting you, they'd be so damn passive? Eh? ...

"Tell me: You think there's a reason they love to call us niggers? The answer is, yes! —and it's because too many of us act like we always-scared NIGGROES!"

Rhonda snapped at her supervisor: "HOW DARE YOU SPEAK TO ME LIKE THAT? Do I look like a 'niggroe' to you? DO I LOOK LIKE A NIGGER TO YOU?" (And in the office the sound of the air-conditioning filtered into the awkward silence.)

"Oh no! —he didn't!" Chanise Griffin howled and whooped: "OH NO HE DID NOT CALL HER THAT!"

Rhonda heard none of it through a strange discordance in her head. She turned away from her supervisor's desk, bee-lined to her own amid dropped jaws, snatched up her purse and walked out.

Soon after, someone reported to Human Resources that Kevin Carter called Rhonda Brown a nigger and that she was so upset she went home. The head of Human Resources reported the alleged incident to Senior Management before calling in Fred Carmichael, Kevin's boss, and tasked him to do an in-depth investigation of what took place in the main office.

Fred Carmichael knew he'd have to fire Kevin if what he was accused of turned out to be true. Fred realized that whatever took place between Rhonda and Kevin happened just after he, Fred, had chewed him out for security being so lax in the kitchen where they were losing inventory. He remembered how Kevin had left looking angry enough to explode. Maybe he did explode on Rhonda. But would he call her the N-word? Fred Carmichael sighed. Not Kevin. He's not stupid.

"Who lodged the complaint?" Carmichael had asked the head of Human Resources.

"We're keeping that confidential," she said, chuckled, shook her head, and added with a dry smirk: "But I'm sure you can guess who it is."

He waited now for Kevin to enter the office. A knock on the door; he took a deep breath. "Come in."

Kevin entered and sat before being asked to and met his boss's eyes squarely. "It's not true. I left here, went back to my office, saw Rhonda raising the temperature on the Thermostat and I snapped at her." He shook his head. "I was wrong and apologized immediately. ... She got off on me and..." Kevin shrugged. "She walked out."

"You never called her the N-word."

"No. I just tried to apologize for snapping at her. Whoever accused me of calling her a nigger is a dirty liar, Fred; and it's not Rhonda; she won't do that!"

"It wasn't Rhonda."

"I know who it is."

Fred Carmichael nodded and added casually: "Kevin ... if this thing goes against you, you're toast. You know that, don't you?"

Kevin Carter cursed below his breath. "So, what happens now?"

"When Brown comes in tomorrow, we'll know."

Chanise Griffin called Rhonda's home that night. Her husband answered and handed the phone to her.

"Hello?"

"This is Chanise."

"Hi, Chanise...."

"Girl, at last, you'll get justice for yourself and for the rest of us!"

Rhonda's brows furrowed. "What are you talking about, Chanise?"

"He called you a nigger—and they're going to fire his arrogant ass!"

"Who called me a nigger, Chanise?"

Silence.

"Chanise? You there?"

"Didn't Kevin call you nigger this afternoon?"

"No ... he didn't."

"What you mean he didn't? —Wait a minute! —did he call you before me and butter you up? —promised you something?"

Rhonda was baffled. "What are you saying, Chanise?"

"Okay! So that's the way it's going to be?" Chanise Griffin snapped. "So, you're going to hang me out to dry, huh? —your own people? But I should have known—and Pat was right: Caribbean people are Caribbean people, and Americans are Americans—we're not the same!"

Chanise ended the call.

Rhonda, bewildered, turned to her husband foraging for something to eat in the refrigerator.

"I heard her all the way here," he said casually. "Woman's pissed. What was that, about?"

"Honestly, Gordon? I don't know."

"You will tomorrow. But don't take no shit from none of them!"

Rhonda parked her vehicle and opened the door to get out. She saw a small group of African American kitchen workers, mostly young men and a tall middle-aged man, by the large dumpster. They spotted her and stopped talking.

"Morning, Guys!"

Each in the group murmured 'Good morning.' The tall middle-aged man in an apron started toward her; the rest followed.

"Good morning," the tall guy said, his hands loosely clasped before his mid-section. "Can we speak to you, Miss Brown?"

"Of course, guys—how can I help you?"

"We heard what the white boy Kevin called you, and we knew..." He quickly indicated the others in his small group. "...that in time he'd have revealed his true self."

"What do you mean?" (Rhonda's mind never stopped reeling from last night when she learned that Chanise thought that Kevin called her a nigger. Here she was confronting it again. Clearly, what Chanise thought took place at Kevin's desk constituted Chanise's deliverance—her chance to see the last of Kevin Carter; now, here were these guys.)

The lead guy continued: "His people are all Klans-people up in Winder. Shit! They dress in white sheets; wear the pointed hoods and everything!"

(*OH, MY, GOD!* Rhonda thought.)

"The first time Obama won, Kevin's daddy set his two pit bulls on a Jamaican neighbor—a woman he thought was celebrating too much—"

Rhonda's eyes flared. "OH MY GOD!"

"One tore out a chunk of her leg before her son heard her screaming and rushed out with a machete. He saw the attacking dogs and managed to kill one and wounded the other."

"And the first thing those cracker cops did was arrest the Jamaican guy!"

"Oh my God—so what happened?"

"Kevin pulled some strings, and everything calmed: The woman was paid a lot of money and his father didn't serve time."

"Settled out of court."

"Yeah. They say Kevin Carter is associated with 'old money'. Someone here is always covering for him despite him always screwing up. You think he'd still have that job if he was one of us? Shit!"

"Let's see how that woman in Human resources and his boy Carmichael cover his ass now!" grumbled a stocky guy in the group.

The tall man continued: "Miss Brown, what he called you amounts to a hate crime; violation of your civil rights—"

"With your word and Chanise's against him? That racist mother-fucker's gone, baby!"

The tall man looked coldly at the speaker. "Watch your language, Wright! We have a lady here!" Then he turned back to

Rhonda: "But Miss Brown ... the moment you get in, Carmichael will call you and Kevin to have a talk. Make sure you tell it like it was and force them to fire him! He's always getting away with stuff in this place! ... Anyway, Miss Brown, we don't want to make you late."

"I'm actually fifteen minutes early—but I have to make this call, guys."

They retreated, looking 'pumped', then disappeared inside.

Rhonda Brown sat in her SUV, reached inside her bag for her phone, and simply held it limply in her lap. She couldn't believe what was happening. How did she end up in this? She needed to call Gordon.

Rhonda entered the office. Chanise, looking like a swollen toad, said nothing to her. Rhonda glanced around; everyone focused very hard on what they were doing.

Kevin entered just after she did. "Morning, Rhonda," he said.
"Good morning!"

Immediately after, Fred Carmichael appeared in the doorway. He asked Rhonda and Kevin to accompany him to his office.

"Rhonda..." Fred Carmichael began, "I'm going to get directly to the issue at hand..."
"Yes, Mr. Carmichael."
"Did Kevin call you the N-word."
Rhonda's brows furrowed. "I don't understand—what do you mean the 'N-word'?"
Rhonda was sure she saw Fred Carmichael squirm in his seat.
"Miss, Brown ... did Mr. Carter call you a 'nigger'?"
She grinned inside as she heard herself say, "Yes."
"You're lying!" Kevin Carter exploded. "I never called you a nigger!"
"YES! YOU DID! —CHANISE HEARD YOU!"
"Mrs. Brown—"
She turned sharply on her director. "What, Mr. Carmichael? Is it time for the lets-protect-Kevin-Carter dance? —No! He called me a nigger! —and if management does not fire him, I'm

going to sue the—" A sharp rap on the driver's side window and a voice brought her out of her daydream.

"Hi, Rhonda —the cake stand you returned? I got it—thanks."

"Morning, Bridgette—you're welcome."

"Thanks."

Rhonda entered the office. Everyone was looking at her except Chanise.

"Morning, Rhonda," Kevin said.

"Morning."

"We have to go to Fred's office."

She accompanied him to the director's office. There Rhonda recounted to Fred Carmichael, everything that happened the previous afternoon.

"So, Rhonda, Kevin did *not* call you the N-word."

"He did not. I was angry after he shouted at me, so I asked him if he thought I was a nigger. I'm sure someone must have heard that and thought he called me the N-word. No; Kevin never called me a nigger."

"Thank you, Rhonda," Kevin murmured.

"You're welcome," she said flatly.

"Well..." Fred Carmichael said and sighed in relief. "Rhonda ... thanks for clearing this up."

When they got back to the office, Kevin Carter, set the temperature on the Thermostat at a level tolerable for Rhonda Brown. The only person in the office who registered any discomfort to the rise in the office's temperature was Chanise Griffin. "God! —it's hot in here!" she muttered below her breath and began fanning herself profusely.

But Rhonda wasn't minding Chanise; Rhonda was clearing the single drawer of her desk—transferring the few personal items from it to her purse as the echo of the conversation she had with her husband in the parking lot played back in her head:

"Listen, Babes... Do you think my heating and air-conditioning business is doing good—that it's successful?"

"Yes..."

"And how many rental apartments we own?"

"Three."
"And why are you working—is it because you have to work?"
"No, it's because I want to work." She started chuckling because she saw Gordon's drift.
"So, Babes ... just do what you feel you should do."

Rhonda Brown got to her feet, walked past Chanise—food-messy at her desk, avoided Pat, the Southern woman with the prominent ass, past Charles whom most thought was bipolar, turned the thermostat down to sixty degrees, walked out the door to the parking lot; got into her Lexus SUV, and drove away.

Now to the stories behind the above story. I once worked at a newspaper in Hackensack, New Jersey where there was an altercation on the mailroom floor. A black immigrant worker who used to be a doctor back in his country felt he was being spitefully targeted by a white, junior supervisor who ordered him to sweep the floor. Let's call the supervisor, Buddy—and yes, he *was* an arrogant piece of work; and let's call the immigrant guy David. So, David turned to Buddy and snapped, "Who the hell do you think you're talking to Buddy? Do I look like a negro to you?"

Nearby, there was an African American woman who hated Buddy with a passion. She heard what she wanted to hear, darted to the mail room manager's office and lodged the complaint that Buddy called David a 'nigger.' And just like that, there was a crisis. Buddy stood to be fired if it turned out to be true. The mailroom manager called David to her office. When he got there, he found a troubled Buddy. The manager explained what was going on: that there was a report that Buddy called him a nigger and that upper management was set to fire Buddy. David then told the manager that nothing of the sort happened and explained what transpired. He then volunteered to go up to upper management and clear Buddy of all charges. The manager said, "If you would do that—why not?" So, David sat with upper management, cleared up the situation, after which Buddy and David became great friends. This became the subplot for *The Thermostat*.

Rhonda having a hard time in the office because it's always too chilly for her is my girlfriend's story. She dresses in layers to be warm and walks to work with a portable heater which she keeps under her desk. One night, lying in bed and gazing at the ceiling, I thought of a casual discussion I heard the day before—about whether there's scientific evidence that proves Caucasians have a higher tolerance for cold temperatures than other races, especially blacks. I found myself thinking about the chill in my girlfriend's office and turned and looked at her purring in sleep. I thought, *What would happen if one day she just gets up, goes to the thermostat, and turns up the heat?* I concluded that such an action might cause conflict. And just like that, I was thinking of David, the ex-doctor and Buddy the young white supervisor ... of the African American woman who ran to the manager's office. And slowly, the plot of *The Thermostat* came together.

- Most of my stories are spawned from real-life incidents drawn from my life experiences and the life-experiences of other people. I also get ideas from something I might see in the news or read in the news.

- At other times I think of something that bothers me—consumes me, like bigotry, prejudice or racism leveled against specific demographics or individuals. Times like those, a part of me aches to say something about it—to speak out about it. In that mode, I would think, *What kind of story can I put together to say how I feel?* I must tell you, however, that I find stories like those difficult to write. A fiction writer never wants to come over as if armed with an obvious agenda—as if spouting propaganda from a soapbox. The depth of your feeling or angst about a specific subject might be deep and consuming, but despite this, you the writer should always go over to your readers as a storyteller and nothing else. Of course, weave your deep stuff into your story; let your readers sense, after a damn good tale, that there was something else in it that makes them think.

- I also use the very popular 'what-if' approach to get plot-ideas churning in my head. (I touched on the 'what-if' method in **Convo # 5**.) The following is an illustration of how it works: You're sitting at your writing desk. You have a view of the local street running by. You gaze out there and think: *WHAT IF the middle of the street begins to vibrate, collapses inward, multiple horns of something appear, and then a mythical dragon-like something explodes into the neighborhood?* Or, you wake, go to the bathroom; look in the mirror and you think, *What if one morning I were to watch in this mirror and something like an alien is looking back at me?* No doubt about it, the 'what-if' prompt gets the creative juices flowing. It is also not new; it might have been something like it that prompted Frans Kafka to come up with the plot for his classic story, *The Metamorphosis*, in which a clerk wakes one morning and discovers he's been transformed into a cumbersome and repulsive beetle of some sort. The 'what-if' approach might also have influenced the screenplay *Watermelon Man* in which a popular, suburban white guy awakens one morning, looks in the bathroom mirror and discovers that overnight he has turned into an African American and is thereafter rejected by his neighbors and coworkers.

With any of the above methods, I would advise you to make copious notes and do short fictional try-outs to see if it's something you can run with. I will caution you, however, that some ideas are harder to develop than others. I have started many stories and later discovered I wasn't matured, mentally or creatively, to finish. The good thing is, I keep ideas for stories in a file on my desktop. Every now and again I'd visit some of those ideas and discover, to my excitement, that I can proceed with and finish some of them.

There are also times when I would start writing a piece—not knowing where it's going and allow its characters, once they are well defined, to determine how the plot will develop and where the story will go. (In CONVO #2, I created a few illustrative paragraphs about a made-up character with the name Janice who stops at a gas station on the way to pick up her daughter from ballet class.) Later, I reread the bit about Janice, and she began to take on a life of her own. So, after leaving the gas station, I decided to drive with her to pick up her daughter—and afterward, see where Janice's story would lead me.

Lousy Cat

By Harold A. Bascom

Janice Tapper pulls into the gas station with the 7-Eleven convenience store attached and drives readily to a vacant pump. She switches off the engine of her aging Toyota Camry, gets out, and begins filling the tank for the rest of the week. *By the time I arrive at Case's ballet class, it should be over.*

The insistent sound of a jackhammer or something makes her look toward the highway running past. Over it, the sprawling commercial complex where she hopes she'd be able to find a job takes shape. It's going to be a craft store. She has researched the company's website and has applied for a position there in the hope of leaving her job as a night waitress.

She thinks of 'Miss Glenda' the retired African American librarian who once lived in the apartment immediately below hers and kept Casey until she got home. Now that Glenda has been evicted, Janice finds it worrisome that when she's at work, her daughter is home alone until after eleven. Janice needs to find a job that would give her the choice of an early shift. That way, she'd be home soon after her daughter gets in from school.

'Miss Glenda' was a soft-spoken woman who used to work at the local community college. After the apartment complex was bought-over, the new management wasn't sympathetic with senior tenants who were finding it hard to make ends meet. There were a few times Janice loaned 'Miss Glenda' money to help keep a roof over her head. But then the new owners raised the rent. Keeping up the payment became extremely difficult for her and she was evicted. *Where's 'Miss Glenda' now?*

The pump clicks; Janice gives the handle a few squeezes for good measure then hangs up the hose and closes the car's gas cap. She gets back in the driver's seat.

"You know you shouldn't do me like that, Craig!" someone chortles.

Janice looks over to the entrance of the 7-Eleven. An obese woman is leaving as she eats a slice of pizza and speaks loudly on her cellphone. Janice's stomach growls. She realizes she hasn't eaten since this morning. She sighs, reaches for her handbag, gets out, and—wary of creepers—locks the door behind her.

She enters to the immediate aroma of pepperoni and looks around at the shelves of colorful knickknacks. She picks up a pack of Oreos for Casey and joins the very short line to the cashier. Her eyes fall on the one-point-six-billion-dollar lottery sign next to the cash register.

At the counter, she buys a cheeseburger, a soda, and then like an afterthought, a lottery ticket.

"Reminds me! I need to get one of those," mutters an elderly female voice behind her. "You don't have a ticket, you don't have a chance!" Soon after, the voice mumbles regretfully, "Damn! I only have enough cash on me to buy a soda!"

Janice turns to a petite African American woman. "Don't worry, I'll get one for you."

"Oh! Thank you! Thank you, Honey! You're an angel. God bless you. ..."

"Don't worry about it," Janice says, smiling.

The woman takes out her cell phone. "Let me take a picture of you, Honey...."

"Okay." Janice freezes.

The woman takes the picture. "I like keeping pictures of kind people...."

Janice laughs. "Thank you."

At last Janice drives into a yard with a red-brick bungalow in the shadow of huge trees. The front door opens framing her daughter and Mrs. French, the dance teacher. Janice gets out the car and Casey, smiling, starts toward her.

"Hi, Mom!"

"Hi, Case; there's some 'Oreos' between the seat for you. I need to speak to Mrs. French.

Janice climbs the brief stair to the standing woman. "A word with you, Mrs. French?"

"Come right in, Mrs. Tapper." The willowy woman turns back into the building, part of which has been converted to a dance floor.

They sit in a corner arranged like a little office.

"Casey may have to stop coming to classes, Mrs. French."

"Why? —She's quite good! Casey's the best I have."

"I can't afford it any longer. ... As a twelfth-grader, there are her SAT-prep classes to pay for, and so much more. I'm really struggling."

"What about this: I'm going to let her continue for free until I close for the winter."

Janice is taken aback. "You would, Mrs. French?"

"You don't have to tell her. She's a proud young woman."

"Oh my God! —Thank you. I won't forget this, Mrs. French."

"That's okay, my dear; with some of us, it's not all about money."

Back in the car, Casey looks curiously at her smiling mother. "You look happy."

"Am I not always?"

"Nope." Casey rakes the cream off an 'Oreo.'

They start home. Soon they are driving past the gas station with the 7-Eleven.

"Mom, I have to tell you something, but don't get mad."

"About what? That you called your father and asked him to pay for your SAT Prep classes?"

Casey's brows knit. "He told me he wouldn't tell you about it!"

Janice shakes her head. "Don't know why you had to go and do badly the first time on that test."

"Jeeze, Mom! Let's not go there again."

"He called me to say he'll be trying to help you—at least with part of it."

They slow then stop for a red light. "I really hope his wife would allow him to help you," Janice says.

"She's nasty! I don't like her!"

"What's *that* about, Casey?"

"I told him about those guys in the apartment over from us and asked him if he can pick me up, so I can stay with him on those days when you come home after eleven—that he can take me back to our apartment after you're home."

"And?"

"He said his wife might not like it." Casey's brows furrow. "He said that she acts stupid sometimes—as if she's jealous of me." She looks at her mom. "I'm his daughter! Why should she be jealous of me?"

"I don't think it has anything to do with you. Your father was always weak!"

"Cut Dad some slack, Mom," Casey mutters and takes out her I-phone.

"Don't worry, Case. Something will work out."

"Because you have a good heart," Casey says chuckling. "Okay, Mom."

She sticks earbuds into her head and ignores Janice for the rest of the ride home.

They pull into the compound with their apartment unit. Teenage boys take turns shooting a basketball into a portable basketball hoop in the parking lot of the apartment building over from Janice's.

Between the young men is a tall mulatto boy Casey has never seen before. She climbs out of the car. He stops shooting and just looks at her as he bounces the ball casually.

Janice gets out and sees the young man staring at her daughter. "For Christ-sake, Casey! Stop staring at whoever that fool is and help me with the groceries!"

He winks at her and pouts her a red-lipped kiss.

"Who's he? I've never seen him around here before," says Janice as she walks behind Casey to their apartment door.

"A few new families have moved in over the last week. Maybe he's from one of them," says Casey.

"Don't like the looks of him! Looks arrogant. Wish I didn't have to live like this!"

"Don't worry, Mom. This won't be forever."

Janice rests the mail on the little table by the front door. She rests the lottery ticket there too.

Casey takes it up. "What are our chances, Mom?" she chuckles.

Janice laughs too as she opens the latest late-rent reminder from Central Office. "One in three hundred million."

"The drawing's tonight. You never know the luck of a lousy cat, Mom."

"Yeah right," says Janice, dryly, thinking that she'd have to ask her sister Sarah to help her with the rent *again*.

She hears footsteps outside ... voices in the apartment that, up to this morning, was empty. Casey, Oreo cookie between her teeth, comes out wrapped in a bath towel. "Someone next door?"

"So it seems." *I wonder who it is—what kind of people?* Janice thinks.

Casey returns to the bedroom. Soon the hissing from the shower comes out to Janice.

"Mom! The faucet's handle broke off on the bathroom sink!"

"I know! I called maintenance. They'll fix it!"

The bump-bump-bump along with the jibes of young men seep in from the improvised basketball court. Janice thinks of the mulatto boy. What if one night, when Casey's alone in the apartment, he comes over? What if he did with some of his friends? What if they break in?

There had been a few crimes in the complex before the management changed and the rental cost to the units went up considerably. Maybe things are better now, but there are still elements Janice considers unsavory that linger.

She thinks of the apartment next door where it seemed new tenants have moved in. She hopes whoever they are would not be like the last couple. There used to be the unmistakable stink of weed seeping from under their door. Janice was even sure the smell lingered in her apartment. She remembers that long-ago day when she came home with Casey and there was a pair of cop cars downstairs her apartment building. And then she saw the couple being brought out in handcuffs.

Later that night, Janice is making a salad. Casey comes out in pajamas and settles on the sofa before the TV. She reaches for the remote. "The lottery will be drawn in a minute, Mom."

"You have the ticket?"

"Yes..." Casey waits with a pen.

Soon the numbered balls begin to fall and then it is all over. Casey sighs. "We didn't win."

"Oh well..."

The next morning Janice and Casey emerge from their apartment and see their new neighbor for the first time. He sits in a wicker-weave chair off the side of his door. A diminutive, middle-aged Latino with the face of a hawk. He smiles to see them but only with his lips. His eyes are sad.

"Good morning," Janice says cheerily.

"Good morning," Casey mutters.

"Good morning," the man replies. "I'm your new neighbor. My name is Cortez; you and your daughter will have no trouble from me."

"I'm happy to know that—and neither will you have any problems from me or my daughter. My name is Janice."

The man nods. "Thank you, Miss Janice."

"Bye," says Janice.

They walk to the car and get in. Janice stares vacantly at a balcony with a dusty grill next to a pot of shriveled plants. She chuckles and shakes her head. "Now we're living next to a guy who looks like a hit man for a drugs cartel." She sighs. "I need to talk to your father—whether his new, young wife likes it or not!"

"What about, Mom?"

"Casey...this place is not good for you. Whoever was that boy staring at you yesterday and now we have this creepy guy next door." She sighs. "I have to work tonight and for some reason, I feel very concerned."

"I'll be okay," Mom. "I lock the door and open it only when you call from the car and say you're here in the parking lot. I'll be okay."

"Okay." Janice starts the car.

Casey checks the news on her I-Phone. "Wow!"

"What?"

"One person has won that lottery!"

"Well," says Janice, waiting to turn right and onto the main street from where they live, "God bless whoever it is."

Casey, brows furrowed, finally turns the page of the physics text, when she hears a gentle rapping at the door. She puts down her pen and looks at the digital clock on the partition to the kitchen. It is a little after ten. The rapping is now louder. Who could it be? Her Dad? It could only be her dad. She tiptoes to the door.

"Is that you, Dad?"

There's no answer. The rapping comes again—slow and firm. She hears the neighbor's door open, and then the voices:

"You're her Papi?" Mr. Cortez says.

"Fuck you, old man!" a young voice says.

"Fuck me? You wanna fuck with this, Holmes?"

Footsteps stumble away and down the stair. And then there's silence.

Casey calls her mom immediately after and tells her what has happened. Janice says she's on the way home.

Janice hurries to her apartment. Her breathing is tight. She sees her neighbor in his chair off the side of his door. Across his knees is a long-bladed knife.

He bows his head and says goodnight.

"What happened, Mr. Cortez?"

"There was a young man at your daughter's door. But he won't come back again. I was waiting here until you came home." He stands. "Now I can sleep. *Buenas Noches*, my neighbor." He starts in.

"Thank you...."

Janice enters her apartment and hugs her daughter—tells her what she found out.

Casey is incredulous. "He was sitting out there waiting for you to come home?"

"Yes; he was. There was a long knife across his knees. Oh, my Gawd."

"Maybe that's why whoever it was, ran!"

"You have a protector," Janice says and sighs despondently.

"What's it, Mom?"

"The manager didn't think I should have left." She shakes her head. "Told him I had to leave."
"You think you can lose your job there?"
"I hope not, Case."
"I'm so sorry, Mom."
"It's okay."

One week later, Janice Tapper loses her job as a waitress. Her sister, Sarah, volunteers to pay the rent until she finds another job. Sarah also pulls a few strings and Janice lands a position in Housekeeping at the nearby hospital. What she makes there, however, isn't enough to hold onto the apartment, so, she gives it up and puts her stuff in storage.

She and Casey move into an extended-stay hotel where they live for one month before Sarah hears about it and was pissed. She berates her sister for always having had too much Gawddamned pride. "How dare you take my beautiful niece to live in a place like this? Huh?"

Sarah makes Janice and Casey move in with her. They settle in her basement. It is much better for Casey than where they were—where it was difficult to study.

Casey's dad doesn't help her with SAT prep classes, but she studies on her own and passes it, anyway. She starts university with the help of Financial Aid and begins to do exceptionally well—determined to be the best she could be in order to find a great job and help her mother—to show her father that they would more than survive—that she and her mother would live.

The new craft store opens at last, but Janice isn't hired. She stays on at the hospital and on day-offs, works part-time at the local dollar store.

One midday, Janice is eating alone outside of the hospital's cafeteria when a co-worker rushes out. "Janice! You're on TV!"

Janice laughs. "Me? On TV? —You mean there's someone on TV that *looks* like me."

"No. Janice Tapper—you!"
"Elaine, what are you talking about?"
"Come quickly!"

Janice enters the area and there is a photograph of herself on a split screen with the caption below: 'Call station.' There's also a number. On the other side a talk show with the host sitting over from a petite, elderly, well-coiffured African American woman with heavy make-up.

Janice's hands fly to her mouth. "Oh, My God!" she blurts. It's the woman she bought the lottery ticket for at 7-Eleven store at the gas station!

"Tell us what happened that day," the host says to the woman.

"Kindness happened that day. I was behind her when I realized that I hadn't enough to buy a lottery ticket..."

"Oh, my Gawd!" Janice gasps.

"My granny taught me to be grateful," says the woman.

"And you need to thank this woman."

"Yes, but in a very special way."

"What way is that?"

"I want to share some of my winnings with her."

"With a mere stranger?

"Well, wasn't that what I was to her when she helped me?

"But you won the one-point-six billion lotteries almost six months ago. Why now?"

"I had a dream about her last night; and in that dream things weren't good for her. She was crying her heart out. It moved me to do this."

"Okay..."

"Yes... the love of Jesus moved me to do this."

"And how much of it you want to share with the unbelievably lucky Janice Tapper?"

"Ten million."

Cheers break out aback the set. A new camera angle shows members of the floor crew clapping.

Clapping breaks out on the cafeteria floor too.

"Make the call, Tapper!"

Janice takes up her cell phone. Her hand trembles.

She thinks of her daughter, Casey...

Of her old neighbor, Miss Glenda...

Of Sarah, her sister...

Of her new neighbor, Mr. Cortez...

Of Mrs. French, the dance teacher...

Of Mitch, the handicapped busboy at the restaurant who told her he'd miss her after she was let go...

And of the quiet Peruvian woman at the dollar-store who was willing to share her lunch with her....

Janice nervously thumbs the numbers below her picture on the TV screen.

"Channel twenty-one, the Good-News Scene—how may we help you?"

"Hello?" Janice says, cautiously. "Yes, my name is Janice Tapper...."

Someone hugs her as tears stream down her face.

Now, let me tell you about the location for the above story, its inspirational foundation, its outline, and a bit about why I chose a single mom as its protagonist. When I made up the 'Janice excerpt' for CONVO #2, I imagined the scene at a gas station in Loganville, a city in North-Central Georgia where I live and where the entire story is set.

As for what inspired it: I have always been intrigued about people who win mega lotteries and wished that more reached out to help the less fortunate in their life-circles. The question that sparked the plot was, *'What if one kind stranger buys a lottery ticket for another, and that ticket goes on to win an amount seemingly-impossible-to-spend? Would that winner remember that selfless stranger who bought that ticket?* And so, I set out to put together a story about selflessness and gratitude and the need for us to recognize that beyond skin-pigmentation pretentions and bullshit, we're all the same: just humans.

As for the structural outline, I chose to build the story around a few telling episodes in a single mother's life as she struggles financially to take care of her teenage daughter and see her through to university without the help of a father who has remarried. My choice to make a single mother the story's protagonist was a deliberate one. This is a category of women I admire for their resolve to be independent and not to buckle.

Much of the details in the above short story are drawn from living with a woman whom I met as a single mother.

In conclusion, writers get ideas for the stories they write from many sources. I have shown you where I get mine. You can get yours from the very sources: life and from the observation of life; from the *what if* prompt and who knows where else. You are a writer; I am confident that one day you will be able to say as I've done in this conversation, "This is how I get my ideas to write..." and proceed to help another new writer just as I hope I have helped you. Peace.

SUPPLEMENT

About My Graphic Illustrations

From the initial idea for this little book I knew I wanted it illustrated and would use my skill as a graphic artist to do so. I also knew that in doing so, a challenge awaited: that of expressing each convo in a single graphic. I worked them all out in the end, however. The following paragraphs reveal my mental process (and a glimpse into my creative technique) that produced each of the illustrations in this book.

CONVO #1: *"How to protect that novel you're writing ..."*

I murmured to myself, "How do I illustrate the concept of the writer-developmental editor relationship?" My first sketch-idea was of a realistic, faceless figure typing earnestly in the foreground with a faceless female figure thinking earnestly as it stood over the shoulders of the typing foreground figure. (The thinking figure symbolized a D.E.) Aback the thinking figure was an irregular background shape of printed text onto which two faces were superimposed: that of a weeping man and a laughing woman. But I hated it because it was old and the composition too traditional. Through the years I did a ton of illustrations that looked like it. I wanted something mind-stirring—crisp, and semi-abstract rendered with a black ballpoint pen. I wanted a bit of collage too—hence the *pasted-on point of a pencil that represents a D.E. It is one of my favorites.*

CONVO #2: *"5 Things you need to take into consideration..."*

Five exclamation marks for five considerations. The idea for this graphic came easy. Using a black ballpoint pen, I rendered a 3-D exclamation mark and followed by duplicating it. I then staggered them between the foreground and background in empty space. I love the minimalist effect.

CONVO #3: *"How to prevent your novel from being tossed..."*

I thought of the cliché 'square peg in a round hole' and knew it would provide me the idea for the visual I sought. I finally came up with the idea of someone lowering an elongated wooden block into a round hole. I went to 'Google Images' where I found letter-blocks. I printed out a few and did a collage-composition to form a single column. The idea for the illustration was to have a hand lowering the column into a dark hole on a printed page. I achieved this by cutting the hands out of card stock, attaching a stiffened bit of string to it and elevating it off the page of printed text. I also elevated the column of letters. I needed shadows for a 3-D effect, so I photographed the entire arrangement in the sun. I then manipulated the image digitally. The process of 'building' this surreal graphic, was a joyful one.

CONVO #4: *"An introduction to choosing points of view..."*

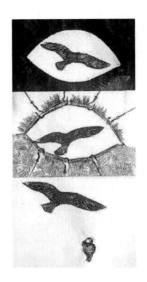

I enjoyed this challenge. "How do I express the first, second, and third person points of view graphically?" It took some mulling over. At last, I imagined someone waking from darkness and seeing a flying seagull. For me, it expressed the perfect visual for first-person subjective point of view, hence the eye opened from a black background. Next was the second-person POV. Since it has the tone of an instructor—a manipulator, I decided that the eye would open by hooks on strings pulling apart the lids so that the flying gull is seen. A graphic representation of the third-person point of view (the omnipresent POV that is all-seeing, all-knowing) was easiest: I simply put myself above the bird and the man looking up at it.

CONVO #5: *"Fiction writing is a craft. ..."*

My first thought for this was, 'Typewriter; keyboard; pens; sheaves of paper—in a toolbox.' After a few quick sketches, the concept looked too cumbersome. In it was not a promise of the designed simplicity I needed. I ended with the hand gripping a pair of pliers—a popular tool of craftspeople—with a pen for one tip and a pencil for the other. Then there is the keyboard which ties in with writing today. I love the simplicity and graphic clarity of this piece.

CONVO #6: "How an acting lesson can help your dialogue..."

If there was one illustration I might do over in the second edition of this book, it would be this one. When I thought of the topic, I saw a stage with actors on it. But I knew I would not place realistic figures there and ended with the head of mannequins.

CONVO #7: *"How to write great descriptive scenes..."*

Coming up with a graphic for this topic was my most daunting challenge. I thought to use high-contrast images of a nose, an eye, an ear, and the tips of fingers, in a montage. To do so, I felt, would be lazy—predictable. The more I thought of it the more I realized that trying to visualize the five senses can easily end cartoonish. One day passed and it wasn't coming to me. On the second day, I thought to myself. 'What is this article about?' and I answered myself: 'How a writer can use the five senses.' I thought of the word 'use' ... and just like that, I saw a hand—like a puppeteer's, with 5 symbols, each representing a human sense, hanging from a string. And I knew I had it!

CONVO #8: *"Would the story of your life make a bestselling..."*

From the beginning, I knew I would use the element of printed type within the highlighted portions of a photo-portrait. I put it together but didn't like it. So, that was scrapped. I began thinking of a

humanoid face—something like an Easter Island kind of image facing itself as in a mirror, with the mirrored image made up of printed type. My aim was to say that an autobiographical work is one that reflects one's life in a document. I knew the concept was spot on. I knew it would work excellently. So, I used a black marker and a ballpoint pen and did one face, then I photographed it. I next imported it into my cellphone's photo-editor and flipped it to create the mirror image. Then I printed out both images onto card stock and cut out both faces. I then pasted printed type on the left side face and blended it into the darkness of the drawing. Finished, I pasted the faces nose to nose on a background, photographed the composition, and enhanced it digitally. I am proud of that piece.

CONVO #9: "How to find the art in rewriting."

This was an easy one for me. Since rewriting is the process of continual improvement of prose—maybe changing something in a sentence of a paragraph here or there until it's the best it can be, I saw repetitiveness, hence the heads of the horse with changes to the manes. This was an easy one for me. The challenge was making it visually interesting.

CONVO #10: "Cliché hunting: How to find them ..."

I decided to illustrate three clichés. From top to bottom, 'Behind every dark cloud, there's a silver lining,' 'A drop in the bucket,' and, 'Like a fish out of water.' I love the surreal mood I caught in the composition.

CONVO #11: *"Where do ideas for the plots..."*

This was another concept that was a bit challenging for me. The visual cliché of the light bulb entered my head. My dilemma was finding a new way to say something old and tired. I wanted to challenge myself to do the light bulb, but a drawing was not going to cut it for me. "Why not use an actual bulb, place it between the pages of an open book, photograph it, and manipulate it digitally?" I whispered to myself. "It would be the only such image in the book, anyway." And that's what I did, and I like it.

ABOUT ME

I am just another unsung writer. I was born in Guyana, South America. My first novel, *APATA: The Story of a Reluctant Criminal*, was published by Heinemann Educational Books of London in 1986. For most of my life, I taught fiction-writing, drama, ran a theatre company, and made a living as a playwright. Currently, I reside in the US state of Georgia where I continue to write and do book reviews of self-published fiction. It was in the latter role that I recognized the need for a book like this and made it a reality. I'm also a painter, a traditional graphic artist and book illustrator.

NOTE TO READER: As a 'thank you' for reading my book, I am prepared to read your novel's synopsis for free and return a critical and objective assessment of it to you. Please make the subject 'READER SYNOPSIS' if you choose to take advantage of the above offer.

My email is, haroldabascom@yahoo.com

Made in the USA
Columbia, SC
23 July 2023